A Calendar of the Warrants for Land in Kentucky, Granted for Service in the French and Indian War

Abstracted by

PHILIP FALL TAYLOR

CLEARFIELD

Excerpted and Reprinted from
*Year Book of the Society of Colonial Wars
in the Commonwealth of Kentucky*
1917

Reprinted
Genealogical Publishing Co., Inc.
Baltimore, 1967
Baltimore, 1975

Reprinted for
Clearfield Company, Inc. by
Genealogical Publishing Co., Inc.
Baltimore, Maryland
1991, 1995, 2001

Library of Congress Catalogue Card Number 67-28596
International Standard Book Number: 0-8063-0327-1

Made in the United States of America

A Calendar of the Warrants for Land in Kentucky, Granted for Service in the French and Indian War

Note: The information contained in this book was excerpted from The Yearbook of the Society of Colonial Wars in the Commonwealth of Kentucky, 1917. Original pagination remains unchanged since the index is keyed to those numbers.

THE FIRST MILITARY SURVEYS
IN KENTUCKY.

It is stated by Collins, and other historians, that the first surveys made in what is now Kentucky were made by a party under Capt. Thomas Bullitt, at the mouth of Beargrass Creek, in July, 1773, who was immediately followed by other Deputy Surveyors working under Col. William Preston, Surveyor of Fincastle County, Virginia.

At that time Fincastle County comprised all of what is now the State of Kentucky with the exception of the eight counties lying west of the Tennessee River, embracing what was later the "Jackson Purchase," bought from the Indians in 1818.

The name of Fincastle County was retained until December 31, 1776, when Kentucky County was formed from a part of Fincastle.

November 1, 1780, Kentucky County was divided into three counties: Fayette included "all that territory beginning at the mouth of the Kentucky River, and extending up its middle fork to the head, and embracing the northern and eastern portion of the present State."

Jefferson then embraced "that part of the south side of Kentucky River which lies west and north of a line begining at the mouth of Benson's big creek, and running up the same and its main fork to the head; thence south to the nearest waters of Hammond's Creek, and down the same to its junction with the Town Fork of Salt River; thence south to Green River and down the same to its junction with the Ohio."

Lincoln County included the rest of the State south of the middle fork of the Kentucky and east of the Jefferson line.

It is a curious fact, that as the junction of the three first counties was at a point in the channel of the Kentucky River opposite the mouth of Benson Creek, the present city of Frankfort embraces land which was originally a part of the three counties, and that the magnificent new Capitol, after so many years of the "Capitol removal question," is now in what was at one time Lincoln County.

January 1, 1785, that part of Jefferson County south of Salt River was cut off and called Nelson County; January 1, 1786, Bourbon was formed from Fayette; August 1, 1786, Madison and Mercer from Lincoln; and May 1, 1789, Mason and Woodford were cut out of Fayette, thus completing the list of nine counties into which Virginia divided the original Kentucky County.

Colonel William Preston was the first Surveyor of Fincastle, and his Deputies, who made the earliest surveys found in the State archives, were James Douglas, John Floyd, Isaac Hite and Hancock Taylor, who were very active in locating land in Jefferson and Fayette Counties in 1774, 1775 and 1776.

Both Taylor and Floyd were killed by Indians; Taylor in July, 1774, and Floyd on April 12, 1783; Douglas and Hite seemed to have escaped the savages and lived much longer than their two comrades.

Hancock Taylor made his will on July 29, 1774, and this was the first legal document, excepting surveys, executed in Kentucky. The original was probated in Orange County, Virginia, and is in the office of the Circuit Clerk of that county. Some years since a relative had a photograph made of the will, and this copy is now in the Kentucky State Historical Society rooms.

Dr. H. R. McIlvaine, Librarian of the State of Virginia, states that about the time Kentucky entered the Union as a sovereign State, June 1, 1792, that "Virginia passed a law giving to Kentucky all the original papers—plats and applicant's descriptions—affecting land in Kentucky, and, so far as the land books are concerned, there are copies in Frankfort of the parts of them concerning Kentucky lands, and only in Frankfort are to be found the original papers, these having been given by Virginia to Kentucky."

The surveys, which were sent by Virginia to Kentucky, are all contained in one cabinet, of ninety metal file cases, containing about sixteen thousand plats and surveys. These papers were evidently boxed up and badly mixed in the shipping, and when received, were indexed just as they were, without being sorted in any manner before indexing; then indexed only in the name of the person for whom the survey was made, disregarding the name of the person to whom the original warrant was issued.

The large majority of surveys were made on Land Office Treasury Warrants, on Pre-emption Warrants and on Settlement Warrants, and while it is known that surveys were made in 1773, none have been found bearing date earlier than March 14, 1774, nor later than May 28, 1789, though these may still be found.

The paper used was generally of very good quality, though many plats are on a slip not over three by eight inches, due to the scarcity of paper; and many of the sheets bear very interesting "water-marks."

Where a sheet of paper as large as our present letter size was used, it has been folded into very small size and so badly creased that many plats are falling to pieces from handling. Unless these papers are opened up and a "flat-filing" system installed, they will, in a very few years, be ruined beyond redemption.

As a general thing, the ink used is still very well preserved, though a few of the surveyors seemed to have used "home-made ink," which is now very pale.

Aside from the value of the surveys, in themselves, there is found a magnificent set of autographs of the old surveyors, of Virginia officials and of men who became famous as officers in the Revolutionary War. Also there are a few copies of wills, deeds, marriage certificates, assignments and affidavits, all of interest to the genealogist and historian.

Altogether it is surprising that such a store of data should so long have been overlooked by the investigators of Kentucky history; but it is a fact that very few people even know of these papers, and those who know have been unable to profit thereby because of the system used in indexing.

FRANKFORT, KY., MAY 20, 1916.

I hereby certify that the Calendar of Surveys made for the Officers and Soldiers of the French and Indian War is a complete and correct list of all such surveys found in the Kentucky Land Office.

PHILIP FALL TAYLOR,

State Archivist of Kentucky.

Earliest Surveys of Land in Kentucky, made as in Fincastle Co., Kentucke Co., Fayette Co., Jefferson Co., and Lincoln Co., Virginia. Principally "By Virtue of the Governor's Warrant Under His Majesty's Proclamation of October 7, 1763." "For Service in the Late War Between France and Great Britain."

From Original Surveys and Plats in the Kentucky Land Office.

Catalogued by Philip Fall Taylor, State Archivist of Kentucky.

Bundles 1-2-3.

No.	Name	Rank	Acres Surveyed	
0,	Philip Love,	Com'd Officer,	2000, July 7, 1774,	By Hancock Taylor, Ass't on waters of Elk Horn Creek, corner to Wm. Peachy's line. Assigned to John Bowman, Isaac Hite, et al.
1,	William Woodford,	Lieut. 2d Va. Reg't,	2000, May 28, 1774,	By Hancock Taylor, on Ohio River 12 miles above Falls at upper end of Large Island—cor. to Hugh Mercer. Fincastle Co. Ass'd to Dr. John Tennant.
2,	Andrew Lewis, Esq.,	Major 1st Va.,	2000, July 8, 1775,	By John Floyd, Ass't, Fincastle Co., on Sinking Creek, 8 or 9 miles from Kentucky River.
3,	Alexander Waugh,	Lieut. 2d. Va.,	1000, May 31, 1774,	By Hancock Taylor, Ass't, Fincastle Co., on Ohio near Falls—cor. to John Connelly's land. Ass'd to Wm. Preston.
4,	Joseph Bledsoe,	Ensign 2d. Va.,	2000 June 28, 1774,	By Hancock Taylor, Fincastle Co., on Kentucke levels—Waters of Elk Horn Creek—cor. to Charles Lewis. Ass'd to Jesse Duncanson—to Hugh Mercer.
5,	Edmund Waggoner,	Subaltern Va. Regt.	1000, June 8, 1774,	By Hancock Taylor, Fincastle Co., on head branches of Beargrass Creek—cor. to John Ashby, to Andrew Waggoner, heir-at-law, Ass'd to Edmund Taylor.

Bundles 1-2-3.

No.	NAME	RANK	ACRES, SURVEYED	
6,	The Right Hon. William Byrd,	Colonel,	1000, June 3, 1771.	By Jno. Floyd, Ass't, Fincastle Co., s. s. of Ohio—cor. William Fleming. Ass'd by M[ary?]] Byrd to John Carter Littlepage.
7,	John Armstrong,	"Sirjant",	200, July 10, 1776,	By John Floyd, Ass't Fincastle Co., on a branch of Licking Creek.
8,	Col. Charles Lewis, dec'd Oct. 10, 1774, to John, Andrew and Charles Lewis, his sons.	Colonel,	2000, June 28, 1774,	By Hancock Taylor, Fincastle Co., on Elk Horn, joins Griffin Peart, John Ashby and Hugh Mercer.
9,	Andrew Lewis,		3000, July 1, 1774,	By Hancock Taylor, Fincastle Co., joins John Lewis, on Elk Horn.
10,	John Lewis,		2000, June 30, 1774,	By Hancock Taylor, Fincastle Co., joins Leroy Griffin, on Elk Horn.
11,	Jacob Boughman,	Soldier 1st Va.,	50, Mar. 31, 1780,	By William McBrayer, Ass't to James Thompson—Lincoln Co., on n. s. Dick's River—joins Thomas Allin.
14,	John Smith,	Capt. in New Levies,	3000, July 13, 1774,	By John Floyd, Fincastle Co., on n. Fork of Elk Horn, cor. to Vaughn, Phillips and Wm. Preston. Ass'd to James Smith—to John Logan—to George Skillern. "John Smith had warrant from Lord Dunmore."
16,	Col. Evan Shelby,	Colonel,	2000, July 16, 1775,	By John Floyd, Fincastle Co., on waters of Elk Horn—cor. to Wm. Preston's land called "Cave Spring."
17,	James Clark,	Lieutenant,	2000, July 8, 1774,	By Jno. Floyd, Fincastle Co. on north branch of Kentucky called Elk Horn Creek—near a very large Buffalo road and crossing. Ass'd to Patrick Henry.
18,	Thomas Bowyer,		1000, June 2, 1774,	By I. Hite, Ass't, Fincastle Co., near Falls of Ohio—cor. to John Connelly and Charles Warrenstaff.

Bundles 1-2-3.

No.	Name	Rank	Acres	Surveyed	
19,	Col. William Christian,	Captain,	1000,	July 17, 1774,	By Jno. Floyd, Fincastle Co., on s. s. waters of Elk Horn, a n. branch of Ky. River—cor. Thomas Barnes.
20,	Samuel Overton,	Captain,	1000,	July 11, 1774,	By Jno. Floyd, Fincastle Co., waters of Elk Horn, on s. s.—cor. to John Ware's land. Ass'd to Col. William Christian.
21,	William Henry,	Lieut. Independ. Co.	1000,	May 16, 1774,	By Jno. Floyd, Fincastle Co., on s. s. Ohio, 3 miles above mouth of Ky. R., joins Peachy's land. Ass'd to Col. William Christian.
22, 23,	John Gilliam, John Gilliam,		200, 200,	Nov. 15, 1775, Nov. 18, 1775,	By Jno. Floyd, Fincastle Co., on a creek which empties into the Ky. about 8 miles above Boonesborough, on the north side.
24,	James Duncanson,	Lieut. 2d Va.,	1000,	June 1, 1774,	by Hancock Taylor, Fincastle Co., on Ohio River, cor. James Southall, Richard Charleton, Hancock Eustace.
25,	William Bradley, also John Blagg,	Capt. 2d. Va., Capt. 1st. Va.,	1000, 1000,	June 7, 1774, June 7, 1774,	By Jno. Floyd, Fincastle Co., on Beargrass Creek—Hugh Allen's survey—on Harrod's Creek, Jno. Floyd's cor. both Ass'd to Col. William Christian.
26.	James Duncanson,	Lieut. 2d Va.	1000,	May 11, 1774,	By Hancock Taylor, Fincastle Co., on s. s. Ohio River, about 6 miles above "Big Meane."
27.	Hugh Mercer,	Col. 3d. Batt., Penna. Regiment,	5000,	May 9, 1774,	By Hancock Taylor, Fincastle Co., on Locust Creek.
28.	George Weedon,	Capt.-Lieut. 2d. Va.,	3000,	June 4, 1774,	By Hancock Taylor, Fincastle Co., on Ohio, about 16 or 17 miles above Falls—to edge of hill above Harrod's Creek. Ass'd to Hugh Mercer.
29.	John Gilliam,		200,	Nov. 18, 1775,	By Jno. Floyd, Fincastle Co., on Creek emptying into Kentucky about 8 miles above Boonesborough.

72

No.	Name	Rank	Acres Surveyed	
33.	David Griffith, also		100, Mar. 11, 1782, 50, Mar. 12, 1782,	By Wm. Montgomery, Ass't to James Thompson, Lincoln Co., on Dick's River, at mouth of Boon's Mill Creek. Ass'd to Jacob Myers.
34.	Thomas Buford, dec'd,		400, Mar. 25, 1783,	By Samuel Grant, Ass't to James Thompson, Lincoln Co., on White Oak Creek. To James Buford, Gdn. to William and Nancy, son and daut. of Thomas, warrant #85.
36.	George Taylor,	Ensign 2d Va.,	1000, June 6, 1774,	By Hancock Taylor, Fincastle Co., on fork of Harrod's Creek. To James Taylor, heir-at-law.
40.	David Robinson,	Officer,	1000, May 16, 1776,	By Jno. Floyd, Fincastle Co., on branch of Ky. River, emptying about 4 miles below Boonesborough.
41.	The Rt. Hon. Wm. Byrd,	Colonel,	1000, May 24, 1774,	By Jno. Floyd, Fincastle Co., on the Ohio about 11 miles below mouth of the Ky. "land called Mount Byrd."
44.	Thomas Buford, dec'd,		400, Mar. 26, 1782,	By Samuel Grant, Ass't Lincoln Co., on Sugar Creek—adj. Scot's land. To James Buford, Gdn. William and Nancy
45.	Richard Omohundro, Francis Drake,	Sergeant, Corporal,	200, May 2, 1774, 200, May 2, 1774,	By Jno. Floyd, Fincastle Co., on the Ohio opposite mouth of Scioto. Both Ass'd by Patrick Henry to Robert Johnson and to Anthony Thompson. Autograph letters with this survey.
46.	George Moffett,		1000, July 5, 1775,	By Jno. Floyd, Fincastle Co. 2 miles from the Ky. River, on waters of Turkey Creek.
47.	Richard Hickman,	Lieutenant,	2000, May 29, 1775,	By Jno. Floyd, Fincastle Co., on Boon's Creek—cor. to William Robinson. To James Hickman, brother, heir-at-law.

Bundles 1-2-3

No.	Name	Rank	Acres Surveyed	
48.	Col. Adam Stephen,	Colonel,	2000, June 29, 1774,	By James Douglas, Ass't Fincastle Co., on n. s. of Ky. River, and n. w. side of Elk Horn Creek, about 8 miles from a remarkable Buffalo fording place, crossing Ky. River. Col. Andrew Lewis's corner. [A large plat with this.] Chain carriers: Jacob Sadusky and Mord'a Batson.
49.	George Frazer,	Lieut. Va. Regt.	2000, July 7, 1774,	By Hancock Taylor, Fincastle Co., on Elk Horn Creek, waters of the Ohio, cor. to Love's land. To Mary Frazer [Fraser] daughter and heir-at-law. Ass'd to Lewis Craig, of Spotsylvania.
50.	William Bell,	Serjeant,	200, June 7, 1775,	By Jno. Floyd, Fincastle Co., on a small branch about 2 miles from the Ky. River—Madison's line—Ass'd to Benjamin Logan—to Nicholas Cary.
51.	Mordeca Debnam,		1000,	By Jno. Floyd, Fincastle Co., on Elk Horn Creek, a branch of the Ky. River. Ass'd to Israel Christian. July 20, 1774.
52.	Col. Adam Stephen,	Colonel,	1000, July 13, 1774,	By James Douglas, Fincastle Co., on n. s. of Ky. River—a branch of the Ohio, on Stehpen's Creek—on n. s. Kentucky, above Dick's River—John Ward's landline of John Poulson. John Willis and Jacob Sadusky, chain carriers.
53.	Col. Adam Stephen,	Colonel,	1000, July 19, 1774,	By James Douglas, Fincastle Co. on n. s. of Ky. River—a branch of the Ohio, on Jessamine Creek—Buffalo Road. William Ballard and Jacob Sadusky, c. c.
54.	Alexander Stephen,	Lieutenant,	2000, July 11, 1774,	By James Douglas, Fincastle Co., on s. branch of Elk Horn Creek, cor. Col. Byrd. "In obedience to a warrant rec'd from his Excellency the Right Hon. John, Earl of Dunmore and Lieut. Gov'r Gen'l of Virginia, to Adam Stephen, hr.

Bundles 1-2-3.

No.	Name	Rank	Acres Surveyed	
55,	Col. Adam Stephen,	Colonel,	1000, May 23, 1774,	By James Douglas, Fincastle Co., on s. s. of Ohio, 3,570 poles above mouth of Kentucky River.
56,	Mordeca Debnam,		1000, July 25, 1774,	By Jno. Floyd, Fincastle Co., on Elk Horn Creek. a n. branch of the Ky. R., about 20 miles from the mouth of the Kentucky River—cor. John Draper—Ass'd to Israel Christian, to John Boyd.
57,	John Waller,	Lieutenant,	1000, May 31, 1774,	By Hancock Taylor, Fincastle Co., on the Ohio, 240 poles above mouth of Beargrass Creek—James Southall's line—Ass'd to Alexander Waugh—to Hancock Taylor—to Zachary Taylor, his heir-at-law. ["This land was surveyed by Hancock Taylor, signed, Wm. Preston, S. F."]
58,	James McDowell, dec'd,		1000, June 14, 1775,	By Jno. Floyd, Fincastle Co., on s. fork of Licking Creek—Hugart's land.
59,	George Moffett,		1000, July 10, 1775,	By Jno. Floyd, Fincastle Co., on waters of Elk Horn Creek.
60,	Zachary Taylor,	Serg't 2d Va.,	200, June 17, 1774,	By Hancock Taylor, Fincastle Co., on a branch of the Ky. River, which emptys at the Great Crossing, being the waters of the Ohio.

Bundle 4.

81,	Charles Tompkins,		100, May 3, 1780,	By James Douglas, County of Kentucky, on waters of Nole Lick Creek, branch of Hanging Fork of Dick's R. Ass'd to John Fox—to Isaac Shelby.
82,	Charles Tompkins,		200, May 4, 1780,	By James Douglas, Kentucky Co., on waters of Knob Lick Creek.
83,	Charles Tompkins,	Subaltern,	200, May 4, 1780,	By James Douglas, Kentucky Co., on Nole Lick Branch of Hanging Fork, both 82 and 83 Ass'd to Fox and Shelby.

Bundles 5 and 6.

No.	Name	Rank	Acres Surveyed
143,	Thomas Booth,		2000, July 17, 1774, By Jno. Floyd, Fincastle Co., on waters of Elkhorn, about 20 miles from Ky. River—John Draper's land—William Russell's land Ass'd to Patrick Coatts—to Hugh Innes—to William Ingles.
250,	John Lightfoot,	Lieutenant,	2000, July 12, 1775, By Jno. Floyd, Fincastle Co., on Elk Horn Creek. Ass'd to David Bell and to John and James Bell, his devisees.
263,	Thomas Buford,	Captain,	924, Apr. 20, 1782, By Samuel Grant, Lincoln Co. n. s. Dick's River—Adj. Wm. Allin, Scott and Davis. To James Buford, Gdn. of William and Nancy, son and dau. of Thomas [See "34 and "44.]
268,	John Craig,		1100, Aug. 23, 1783, By John Bradford, Ass't to George May, surveyor, Kentucky Co., on n. fork of Elkhorn, Military and Treasury Warrant.
459,	Rev. David Griffith,	Surg.'s Mate,	2000, June 5, 1780, By Mer'th Price, "in Kentuckey," near Falls of Ohio, adj. John Connelly, 63 poles from mouth of Beargrass.

Bundle 8.

No.	Name	Rank	Acres Surveyed
309,	Maj. John Field, dec'd,	Major,	1000, Jan. 17, 1783, [Fayette Co.] By Benj'm Field, on dividing ridge between n. fork of Elk Horn and Cain Run—William Bryan's Spring. [Warrant is for 5,000 acres.]
311,	Samuel Edmiston,		200, Mar. 14, 1774, By Jno. Floyd, Fincastle Co., on n. s. middle fork of Holston River.
321,	Thomas Collier,	Subaltern,	1000, Feb. 10, 1783, Robert Johnson, Fayette Co.,—John May's survey—James Suggett's line—Patrick Henry's line. Ass'd to Lewis Craig—to John Craig—to Robert Johnson.

Bundle 8.

No.	Name	Rank	Acres Surveyed	
354,	William Ward,	Subaltern,	2000, July 21, 1781,	By George May, Jefferson Co., 400 acres on lower side of Salt River. Ass'd to Capt. Thomas Rowland—to John May to George May.
361,	Theodosius McDonald,	Ensign,	1000, May 20, 1774,	By Hancock Taylor, Fincastle Co., on Ohio River—cor. to William Henry.
367,	Christopher Best, also Christopher Finnie,	Soldier,	50, June 4, 1780, 50, June 4, 1780,	By James Thompson, in Kentucky, on n. s. of Kentucky River, both Ass'd to Thomas Rowland [George May, surv'r Kentucky Co.].

Bundles 10-11.

No.	Name	Rank	Acres Surveyed	
380,	James Fitzgerald,	Sergt. Byrds Regt.	200, Dec. 17, 1781,	By Wm. Montgomery, Lincoln Co., on a branch of Green R., cor. Cornelius Yeager—to Benj. Pettit's line. Ass'd to William C. Smith. [Warrant #156.]
394,	Jonah Grant, Henry Nevill,	Soldier old Va. Regt. Soldier old Va. Regt.	50, Jan. 9, 1783, 50, Jan. 9, 1783,	By Hubbard Taylor, Lincoln Co., on Kentucky R., Ass'd to Samuel Todd.
415,	Henry Black,	Sold. Col. Byrd's Regt.	50, Dec. 31, 1782,	By Thomas McClanahan, Fayette Co., "on a branch that emptys into the Ky. below the old canoe landing." [Warrant #43.] Ass'd to Sam'l Todd—to John Todd.
421,	Alexander McClenahan,	Capt. in Col. Bouquet's expedition,	1000, Nov. 9, 1782,	By Hubbard Taylor, Jefferson Co., on waters of Green River, Cumberland Road Fork of Sinking Creek, and 1st fork n. w. of said road. Ass'd to Alex'r Sinclair.
539,	Thomas Collier,		1000, Jan. 21, 1783,	By James Garrard, Fayette Co., on Stoner's Fork of Licking.
572,	James Satterwhite,	Private,	50, Jan. 13, 1783,	By Hubbard Taylor, Lincoln Co., s. e. of a survey of 1,000 of Isaac Hite, et al. Ass'd to Lewis Craig—to Edward Darnaby.

Bundles 10–11.

No.	Name	Rank	Acres Surveyed	
574,	Reuben Vass,	Subaltern Stephen's Regt.	500, Jan. 25, 1783,	By James Garrard, Fayette Co., on Stoners Fork of Licking. Ass'd to Thomas Montague—to William Ellis.

Bundles 14–15.

681,	Thomas Walker,	Sold. Capt. Hogg's Co Rangers,	50, Nov. 19, 1781,	By William McBrayer, Lincoln Co., s. s. Dick's R. Ass'd to Francis Kertley and to John Doharty.
751,	Joseph Newnan,	Sold. in Regt. Com'd by Gen'l Braddock,	50, Mar. 1, 1782,	By Wm. Montgomery, Lincoln Co., on s. s. Dick's R. Ass'd to James Barnett. Warrant No. 1090.
768,	Reuben Vass,	Subaltern Byrd's R.	500, Jan. 21, 1783,	By Samuel Grant, Fayette Co., cor. to Lewis Craig. Warrant No. 547.
776,	Reuben Vass,	Sub. Stephen's R.,	500, Jan. 21, 1783,	By Samuel Grant, Fayette Co., on waters of Stoner's Fork, cor. to Benj. Craig, Lewis Craig and Elijah Craig. Ass'd to Thomas Montague. Warrant No. 634.

Bundles 16–17.

808,	Nicholas Sallis, Edward Cary, John Madison, John McClenachan,	Soldier, Subaltern,	1000, Jan. 4, 1782, 1000, Jan. 4, 1782, 1000, Jan. 4, 1782, 1000, Jan. 4, 1782,	By I. Hite, Jefferson Co., on Fern Creek. Ass'd to Sampson Matthews. Warrant No. 348.

Bundles 18–19

Surv. War't.				
847,896,	Justinian Wills,	Sergt. Maj. Byrd's Regt.	100, Mar. 4, 1783,	By Green Clay, Lincoln Co., 'on waters of Sugar Creek—cor. to William Dewitt. Ass'd to Walter Dewitts.
856,848,	Stephen Handcock,	Private,	50, July 23, 1782,	By James Thompson, Lincoln Co., cor. to John Jackson.

Bundles 20-21.

No.	Name	Rank	Acres Surveyed	
883, 22,	Edward Willis,	Private 2d Va.,	50,	Feb. 11, 1783, By A. Eastin, Fayette Co., on Miller's Creek, a big fork of n. Elkhorn. All Ass'd to Joseph Watkins.
23,	Edward Murphy,	Private 2d Va.,	50,	
24,	James Huckstep,	Private 2d Va.,	50,	
25,	Richard Bennett,	Private 2d Va.,	50,	
26,	John Lewis,	Sergt. 2d Va.,	200,	
27,	John Hughes,	Ensign 2d Va.,	1000,	
34,	James Hibbin, dec'd,	Soldier 2d Va.,	50,	[To William Hibbin, heir-at-law.]
34,	Peter Lawson, dec'd,	Soldier 2d Va.,	50,	[To David Lawson, heir-at-law.]
883, 37,	James Baughan,	Soldier,	50,	
37,	George Hancock,	Soldier,	50,	
38,	John Woodson,	Soldier,	50,	
39,	Ambrose Stogle,	Soldier,	50,	
40,	William Walker,	Soldier,	50,	
55,	John Hughes,			
55,	John Williams,			
55,	John Faris,			
55,	Jabez Stecker,			
55,	John Knroughty,		500,	[In all 2,250 acres Ass'd to Joseph Watkins.]
55,	William Saunders,			
55,	James Cawthon,			
894, 623,	Benjamin Temple,	Subaltern Peachy's Batt.,	2000,	Oct. 30, 1783, By Hubbard Taylor, Jefferson Co., on Floyd's Fork. Adjoin. James Taylor's 2,000 a.
898,	Edward Ward,		3000,	July 8, 1774, By James Douglas, Fincastle Co., on n. s. Ky. River, on the head branches of s. fork of Elk Horn—head of Jessamine Cr.

Bundles 22-23.

No.	Name	Rank	Acres Surveyed	
899,	Edward Ward,		2000,	July 12, 1774, By James Douglas, Fincastle Co., on n. s. Ky. River, on the head branches of s. fork of Elk Horn—head of Jessamine Cr.
918, 218,	James Cowhard,	Subaltern,	2000,	Dec. 11, 1782, By Samuel Grant, Fayette Co., on waters n. fork of Elkhorn—William Grant's land. To Jonathan Cowhard, heir-at-law. Ass'd to Joseph Early.

Bundles 22–23.

No.	Name	Rank	Acres	Surveyed	
944,152.	William Vawter,	Lieut. Hogg's Ind. Co.	200,	Jan. 21, 1783,	By James Garrard, Fayette Co., on Stoner's Fork of Licking. Cor to Lewis Craig.
154,	David Thompson,	Serg't Byrd's Reg't.	200,		
478,	George Robinson,	Private Washington's Reg't..	50,		[To William Robinson, heir-at-law.]
485,	William King,	Private Washington's Reg't.,	50,		All Ass'd to Elijah Craig.
975,143,	Thomas Swearingen,		2000,	Feb. 13, 1782,	By Thomas Swearingen, Fayette Co., "on Maney Crossings on a branch of Johnston's fork of Licking."

Bundles 24–28.

No.	Name	Rank	Acres	Surveyed	
987, 31,	James Lankford,	Soldier,	50,	Jan. 2, 1782,	By A. Eastin, Fayette Co., on n. s. of
32,	Joseph Shepherd,	Sold. 2d. Va.,	50,		n. fork of Cooper's Run.—Cor. James
35,	David Harris,	Sold. 2d. Va.,	50,		Heath. All ass'd to Benjamin Bowles
163,	James Harris,	Sold. 2d. Va.,	50,		and Augustin Eastin.
996, 243,	Horatio Gates,	Field Officer,	1000,	Mar. 22, 1781.	By A. Eastin, Fayette Co., on waters of Lee's Creek, on e. s. of Licking—William May's line. Ass'd to Samuel Meredith—to George Clymer.
1001, 931,	James Wilkinson,	Soldier 2d Va.	50,	Feb. 15, 1783,	By A. Eastin, Fayette Co., on Cooper's Run—cor. A. Eastin. Ass'd to Thomas Watkins.
1027, 769,	John Hill,	Sergeant,	200,	Dec. 18, 1781.	By Wm. Montgomery, Lincoln Co., on a branch of Green River—Wm. Montgomery's line. Benjamin Pettits cor.—James Barnet's cor.

Bundles 29–30.

No.	Name	Rank	Acres	Surveyed	
1040, 695,	Joseph Grimsley,	Soldier Byrd's,	50,	Jan. 11, 1783,	By Thomas McClanahan, Jr., Fayette Co., on branch of Huston's Fork. All ass'd to Thomas McClanahan.
696,	John Brunley,	Soldier Byrd's,	50,		
697,	Christopher Fielding,	Soldier Wash'n.	50,		
698,	Patrick Ritchie,	Soldier Wash'n,	50,		
699,	Jno. Baker Turner,	Soldier Wash'n,	50,		
700,	William Poulter,	Soldier Byrd's,	50,		
1019,1109,	Benjamin Gibson,	Soldier Byrd's,	50,	Jan. 13, 1783,	By Hubbard Taylor, Lincoln Co., Joseph McMurtry Stafford's line.

Bundles 29–30.

No.	Name	Rank	Acres Surveyed	
1085,499,	William Fields,	Soldier,	50,	Jan. 5, 1784, By John H. Craig, Fayette Co., on Glen's Creek—Cor. to Richard Young—Ass'd to Thomas Allcock—to Thomas Blanton.

Bundles 31–32.

1134,835,	Benjamin Row,	Soldier,	50,	Sept. 14, 1783, By Samuel Davis, Lincoln Co., on Cobran's Creek, waters of Dick's R., adj. Whitley's settlement.

Bundles 33–34.

1154,281,	Edward Blackburn,	Subaltern,	300,	Dec. 6, 1782, By Charles Morgan, Fayette Co., on a branch of Hickman's Creek. To George Blackburn, hr-at-law. Ass'd to Walker Johnson.
1155,1002,	James Lockheart,	Sold., Capt. Sager's Co.,	50,	Dec. 5, 1782, By Charles Morgan, Fayette Co., on Ky. R., about 3 miles below mouth of Hickman's Creek. Ar. Walker Johnson's.
1146,	James Johnson,	Sold. Capt. Dickenson's Co.,	50,	
1163,105,	John Skelton,	Com. Off.,	200,	Apr. 7, 1784, By Robert Johnson, Fayette Co., on n. fork of Elkhorn, adj. Patrick Henry's—Richard Branham's line.
1170, 32,	Alexander McClanahan,	Capt. Col. Bouquet's Exped'n.,	1000,	Jan. 13, 1783, By Mat. Patterson, Fayette Co., on Mill Creek, a w. branch of Licking. Ass'd to Jacob Lockhart.
215,	Robert McClanachan, dec'd,	Sergeant,	200,	
1203,139,	Henry Nixon,	Soldier Field's Co. (Gen. Forbes' Ex.)	50,	By............Fayette Co., on Rock Bridge Run, a w. br. of Bowman's Creek.
1215,455,	Joseph Bledsoe,	Serg't Washington's,	200,	Mar. 5, 1784, By Richard Young, Fayette Co., beg. on bank of Ky. R., about 2 miles below Benson's Cabbin. Ass'd to John Craig.
459,	Thomas Hidgcock,	Soldier,	50,	

Bundles 35–36.

1216,816,	John Johnson,	Soldier Hogg's Co.,	50,	Sept. 20, 1782, By Robert Todd, Fayette Co., on Kentucky, below mouth of Cedar Run, at McMurtry's Ford. Ass'd to John Parker—to Rev'd John Todd and Robert Todd.

Bundles 35–36.

No.	Acres Surveyed	Rank	Name
1232, ...	1000, June 13, 1775, By John Floyd, Fincastle Co., on Licking Creek.	Lieutenant	William Hugart, ("I certify the above a true copy taken from the records of Fincastle Co., now Montgomery Co., Mar. 11, 1784, John Preston, S. M. Co.")
1235, 84,	500, Dec. 13, 1782, By John Shelby, Jr., Fayette Co., on waters of Hickman's Creek. Issue Shelby and Chesley Callaway, Chn. Carriers; Daniel Boone, Marker.		Evan Shelby,
1241, 71,	200, Feb. 28, 1783, By Matthew Walton, Jefferson Co., on Hog Run, a br. of Beech Fork.	Corporal Byrd's	John Saunders,
1247, 936,	200, Jan. 9, 1783, By Thomas Hutchings, Lincoln Co., on Whitley's Creek. Ass'd to William Stone.	Serg't Byrd's	William Russell,
1255, 397,	200, Apr. 19, 1783, By Ben Pope, Jefferson Co., on s. s. of Beech Fork. Ass'd to Martin Loggins—to Richard Parker.	Corp'l James Green's Co. of Regulars,	Richard Sansome,
1256, 386,	200, Jan. 23, 1783, By Thomas Whitledge, Jefferson Co., on n. s. Beach Fork, above mouth of Sunfish Run.	Corp'l 1st Va.	James Loggins,

NOTE.—From this point on, the surveys are not numbered, but are filed in bundles of about 50 to 75 surveys each, and are indexed by bundle only.

Bundle 37–38.

No.	Acres Surveyed	Rank	Name
Warrant 170,	50, Dec. 13, 1783, By William Daniel, Jefferson Co., on Ohio River, adj. Daniel and Hite.	Soldier Byrd's,	George Rusher,
953,	2000, July 15, 1783, By Philip Phillips, Jefferson Co., on Hincks Run, a br. of Nolin.	Commisary to Peachy's Batalion,	Israel Christian,
1105,	50, ..., By............, Lincoln Co., on waters Dick's R., adj. James Davis—Whitley's Settlement.	Sold. Capt. John McNeelis's Co.,	William Ragsdale.
1077,	50, By Samuel Grant, Fayette Co., on w. s. Hickman's trace, about 1 mile from Hickmn's Creek. Ass'd to James Hogan.	Soldier Byrd's,	Jeremiah Blinford,

No.	Name	Rank	Acres Surveyed
Bundles 37-38.			
Warrant,	Thomas Bowyer,	Officer,	1000, July 16, 1774, By Jno. Floyd, Fincastle Co., on n. s. Ky. River, about 8 miles e. of the head of Elk Horn Creek—Patrick Henry's line—Ass'd to John Howard.
Bundles 39-40.			
Warrant, 387,	Gabriel Throckmorton,	Captain,	500, Nov. 8, 1788, By B. Netherland, Jefferson Co., on E. Floyd's Fork—John Thruston's line—Francis Taylor's cor.—Ass'd to James McCormick—to William Hobday—and all ass'd to John Thruston by Edmund Taylor, power of Att'y.
388,	Gabriel Throckmorton,	Captain,	500,
609,	Edward Foley,	Soldier,	50, By Fayette Co., at the head of a small branch that runs into Glen's Creek, on the n. s.
1209,	George Taylor,	Ensign,	1000, Dec. 9, 1783, By Alex'r Breckenridge, Jefferson Co., near the Ohio—cor. to Edmund Taylor. To James Taylor, heir-at-law, of George Taylor, dec'd. "For Military service in the Va. service in the late war. Certificate of which hath been duly certified under the Hand and Seal of Dunmore.
1210,	Edmund Waggoner, dec'd,	Subaltern,	1000, Oct. 29, 1783, By B. Netherland, Jefferson Co., on Ohio River—Tennant's line. Ass'd to Andrew Waggoner, hr-at-law—to Edmund Taylor.
136,	Charles Lewis, dec'd,	Captain,	1000, Oct. 29, 1783, By B. Netherland, Jefferson Co., on Floyd's Fork.
137,	Charles Lewis, dec'd,	Captain,	1000, Oct. 29, 1873, By B. Netherland, Jefferson Co., on Floyd's Fork.

No., Name	Rank	Acres Surveyed
Bundles 39-40.		
Warrant, 138, Charles Lewis, dec'd,	Captain,	1000, Oct. 29, 1783, By B. Netherland, Jefferson Co., on Floyd's Fork. All to Joseph Jones, Gdn. of John Lewis and Charles Lewis, sons of Charles Lewis, dec'd.
Bundles 41-42.		
544, Thomas Farah,	Sold. Stephen's R.	50, Feb. 26, 1783, By James Kinkead, Lincoln Co., on Scot's Creek, s. s. Kentucky River.
550, Isom Crow,	Serg't Byrd's R.	200, Mar. 12, 1784, By Robert Johnson, Fayette Co., on Dry Creek—Thomas Carnal's line. Ass'd to Elijah Craig and to Robert Johnson.
John McDiffit,	Sergeant,	200, July 20, 1774, By Jno. Floyd, Fincastle Co., on waters of Elk Horn Creek—Anth'y Paul's line.
Nathan Abbott,	Non-Commiss'd,	200, May 20, 1774, By Jno. Floyd, Fincastle Co., on Ohio, in first large bottom below mouth of Scioto. Ass'd to Samuel Meredith.
337, Thomas Morton,		2000, Mar, 12, 1783, By Matthew Walton, Jefferson Co., on n. s. of Beech Fork—Hardin's Creek. Ass'd to Martin Nall.
Bundle 48.		
328, Thomas Lovell,	Drummer,	200, Aug. 24, 1783, By John Handley, Jefferson Co., on Long Lick Creek, formerly Panther Creek. Ass'd to William Fleming.
1008, 1000, William Francis,	Soldier 1st Batt., Royal Americans,	50, July 22, 1783, By Samuel Davis, Lincoln Co.—Logan's Creek, cor. to John Crow. Issued to John Crow.
1009, John Francis,	Sold. 1st Reg't, Reg.,	50, July 22, 1783, Henry Francis, bro. and hr-at-law. Ass'd to John Francis, Jun'r, Ex'r of Henry Francis—then to John Farris.
326, William Fleming,	Ass't Surgeon,	1000, Aug. 25, 1783, By John Handley, Jefferson Co., on Long Lick Creek, formerly Panther.

Warrant No.	Name	Rank	Acres	Surveyed	
Bundle 50.					
	John Wilkins,	Soldier,	50,	Jan. 12, 1783,	By Daniel Boone, Fayette Co., on Two Mile Creek.
	William Branaugh,	[Part.],	500,	Nov. 8, 1783,	By Jeremiah Briscoe, Jefferson Co., on main e. fork of Simpson's Creek.
16.21.	Archibald Buchanan,	Sergt. Capt. Preston's Rangers],	200,	Sept. 8, 1783,	By Wm. McBrayer, Lincoln Co., on w. s. Salt R., adj. James McConn, Sen'r.
47.	William White,	Soldier,	50,		By ____, Jefferson Co., on Beech Fork, Ass'd to Henry Carryer.
48.	Lewis Green,	Soldier,	50,		By ____ Jefferson Co., s. e. Both Ass'd to Abraham Hite—to John Kennedy.
959.	William Smith,	Sergeant,	200,	Mar. 9, 1783,	By Robert Johnson, Fayette Co., on the Ohio, near mouth of Dry Creek, cor. to William Peachy, Ass'd to Cave Johnson.
Bundle 52.					
179.	Thomas Poe,	Soldier,	50,	Feb. 1, 1783,	By Alex'r Breckenridge, Jefferson Co., on Fish Pool Creek and Floyd's Fork, cor. William McConley and Gabriel Jones.
306.	Alexander Finnie,	Qr. Mr. Byrd's R.,	400,		
307.	Alexander Finnie,	Qr. Mr. Byrd's R.,	400,		
308.	Alexander Finnie,	Qr. Mr. Byrd's R.,			
333.	Sylvester Hughes,	Sold. Robert Stewart's Co. Reg's,	50,		
334.	Charles Croucher,	Sold. Washington's Reg't Reg's,	50,		
731.	James Keeling,	Corp'l Washington's Reg't Reg's,	200,		
740.	Samuel Sparks,	Soldier Washington's Reg't Reg's,	50,		
1048.	John Edwards,	Sold. 1st Va.,	50,	Dec. 12, 1781,	All Ass'd to James Francis Moore.
1049.	John Taggart,	Soldier,	50,		By Wm. McBrayer, Lincoln Co., w. s. Salt R.—George McAfee's Settlement.
1050.	Samuel Conner,	Old Va. Reg't,	50,		All Ass'd to William McBrayer.

NO. Warrant	NAME	RANK	ACRES SURVEYED	
Bundle 52.				
349,	Joel Harlow,	Soldier,	50,	Jan. 4, 1783, By I. Hite, Jefferson Co., on Fern Creek.
350,	James Hebdon,	Soldier,	50,	All Ass'd to Sampson Matthews.
351,	Thomas Hill,	Sergeant,	200,	
357,	William Kincade [Kincaid],	Soldier,	50,	June 25, 1782, By Thomas Allin, Lincoln Co., on Wooley's Run, a br. of Paint Lick, Peter Wooley's Cabin.
Bundle 53.				
249,	Christopher Hudson,	Captain,	1500,	Jan. 13, 1783, By Samuel Grant, Fayette Co., on n. fork of Elkhorn — adj. Phillips — Elijah Craig's line, Ass'd to Lewis Craig.
178,	James Parrish,	Soldier,	50,	May 24, 1783, By Robert Johnson, Fayette Co., on Hickman Creek.
251,	John Poindexter,	Sold. Capt. Fox's Rangers,	50,	
300,	William Soudren,	Sergeant,	200,	
476,	Charles Arnold,	Soldier,	50,	
523,	Richard Four Acres,	Soldier, Col. Washington's R.,	50,	All Ass'd to Lewis Craig.
Bundle 54.				
252,	John Thompson,	Sold. Capt. Jno. Faris' Rangers,	50,	Apr. 27, 1784, By Richard Young, Fayette Co., on waters of Glen's Creek, about 2 miles s. of Sam Estill's cabin. Ass'd to William Arnold—Robert Sanders—Lewis Craig.
717,	William Edwards,	Sold. Capt. Steward's Rangers,	50,	
266,	Henry Harvie,	Soldier,	50,	Dec. 23, 1783, By John H. Craig, Fayette Co., on Glen's Creek—Joseph Blackford's line. Ass'd to Jeremiah Craig.
162,	Major General Charles Lee,	Major [par. 5,000Al],	500,	Dec. 19, 1783, By I. Hite, Jefferson Co., on n. fork of Green River, adj. Abraham Hite—cor. Isaac Hite, Ass'd to James Nourse.

Bundle 57.

No. Warrant	Name	Rank	Acres Surveyed	
69, 70,	John Shelby, Sr., John Shelby, Sr.,		500, 500, Dec. 16, 1782,	By John Shelby, Jr., Fayette Co., on w. fork Hickman's Creek—cor. to Isaac Shelby's land.
135,	Phillip Ross,	Lieut. Bouquet's Ex.	2000, Jan. 23, 1784,	By I. Hite, Jefferson Co., joins Joseph Hite—Harrod's Creek.
873,	Barney Riley,	Soldier,	50, Apr. 1, 1780,	By John Ray, Jr., Jefferson Co., about 2 miles above mouth Cox's Creek, on s. s. Salt R.
946,	John Wiley,	Sold. Capt. Dickerson's Rangers.	50, May 31, 1784,	By Isaac Cox, Jefferson Co., on n. s. Beechfork, adjoin Ezekiel Morris and John Phillips. Ass'd to Thomas Rowland.
955,	John Pryor,	Sold. Capt. Preston's Rangers,	50,	
48, 399,	Dominick Moran, Jacob Cheek,	Soldier, 2d Va., Col. Byrd, Sold. 2d Va.,	50, May 31, 1783,	By Wm. Henry, Lincoln Co., on Harrod's Landing Run, Ass'd to John Gilmore.
974,	David Hudson,	Sold. 2d Va.,	50, 50, Jan. 21, 1783,	By Wm. Henry, Lincoln Co., on banks of Dick's R.—Henry Dougherty's cor. Ass'd to David Henderson—to Samuel Shelton.
	Thomas Swearingen,		500, Mar. 24, 1784,	By Van Swearingen, Fayette Co., on n. fork of Licking.
494,	Michael Rice,	Non-com.,	200, Mar. 5, 1784,	By Rob't Johnson, Fayette Co., on the Ohio, at a place called Bullittsburg. Ass'd to Joseph Smith.
156,	James Phillips,		200, Mar. 25, 1784,	By Van Swearingen, on n. fork Licking. Ass'd to Thomas Swearingen.

Bundle 58.

No. Warrant	Name	Rank	Acres Surveyed	
120,	John McClanahan, dec'd,	Subaltern,	2000, Nov. 12, 1782,	By Hubbard Taylor, Jefferson Co., adj. lands of Anderson & Co., on Lick br. of Robinson's Creek, where Cumberland road leaves Robinson's Creek. To John McClanahan, son and heir-at-law.

Bundle 58.

No. Warrant,	Name	Rank	Acres Surveyed	
119,	Larkin Chew,	Lieut. Col. Byrd's Regt.,	2000, Mar. 10, 1783,	By Hubbard Taylor, Jefferson Co., on Green R., 1½ miles from Pittman's Sta. Ass'd to John McClanahan—to John McClanahan, his son and heir-at-law.
450,	John Sampson,	Soldier,	50, Mar. 12, 1784,	By Wm. Steele, Fayette Co., between r. hand branch of Clear Creek, and the Ky.—Samuel Todd's line—Cunningham's line. Ass'd to Ben Rennolds—to Richard Mitchell.
536,	James Gunn,	Captain,	1000, Mar. 16, 1784,	By Alex'r Breckinridge, Jefferson Co., on the Ohio, bet. lands of Griffin & Mercer —hill near Harrod's Creek, s. fork Harrod's Creek, Ass'd to John Madison, Jr.

Bundles 60–61.

847,	John Kinkead,	Sold. Capt. Lewis' Co.,	50, Apr. 5, 1781,	By Wm. Montgomery, Lincoln Co., on waters of Dick's River.
44,	Richard Williamson,	Soldier,	50, Oct. 4, 1780,	By James Kennedy, Lincoln Co.
58,	William Frogg,		2000, Oct. 27, 1780,	By James Hord, D. S., George May, S. Ky. C., Kentucky Co., on s. Cain Run, and n. s. Dick's R.—John Bowman's Settlement—Joseph Bowman's Settlement—Adam Smith's Settlement. Ass'd to Isaac Hite, John Bowman and Joseph Bowman, in Company.
57,	William Bronaugh,		3000, July 21, 1781,	Jefferson Co., on Stewart's Creek, a branch of Beech Fork of Salt R. Ass'd to Doctor John Briscoe—to William Stewart.
184,	James Ryon,	Soldier,	50, Oct. 30, 1780,	By James Hord, Kentucky Co., on waters of Dick's R.—cor. James Smith. Ass'd to John Wilson.

88

No.	Name	Rank	Acres Surveyed	
Bundles 60–61.				
Warrant,	John Ware,	[War't 3000 A],	1000, June 7, 1774,	By Jno. Floyd, Fincastle Co., on the br's of Bear Grass Creek, s. s. br. of the Ohio—cor. William Christian.
23,	Evan Shelby,		500, June 10, 1780,	By James Douglas, Ass't, George May, Surv., Kentucky Co., on waters of the Rowling Fork of Salt R., on the s. s. of the Hunter's Trace—Clay Lick—Cartwright's Creek.
408,	John Hughes, dec'd,	Soldier,	50, Apr. 30, 1781,	Lincoln Co., on Doctor's Fork. Both Ass'd to William Stewart.
640,	John Johnson,	Soldier,	50,	
886,	Edward Gill, Sen'r,	Soldier,	50, June 4, 1780,	By James Thompson, Ass't, Kentucky Co., on n. s. Kentucky R., Ass'd to Thomas Rowland.
	John Dickenson,		3000, July 1, 1775,	By John Floyd, Ass't to William Preston, Fincastle Co., on waters of Turkey Creek, a branch of the Kentucky, about 5 miles from same—Captain Ware's line.
50,	Henry Steel,	Sergeant,	200, Feb. 19, 1783,	By I. Hite, Jefferson Co., on Fern Creek, adj. Sampson Matthews. Ass'd to Abraham Hite, Sen'r.
Bundle 63.				
361,	Christopher Blackburne,	Sergeant,	100, Apr. 1, 1783,	By Hubbard Taylor, Jefferson Co., on Cumberland Road Fork of Sinking Ck. Adj. William Buckner and James Reid. Ass'd to Robert Ware and Philip Buckner.
362,	Christopher Blackburne,	Sergeant,	100,	
443,	Richard Branham,	Sergt. Washington's Regt.,,	200, Feb. 11, 1783,	By Robert Johnson, Fayette Co., on s. s. of North Elkhorn.
Bundles 69–70.				
557,	Thomas Rowland,	[part]	500, Apr. 7, 1784,	By Nath'l Massie, Fayette Co., on main s. Fork of Licking on s. s.—John Townsdel's line—William Wood's line.

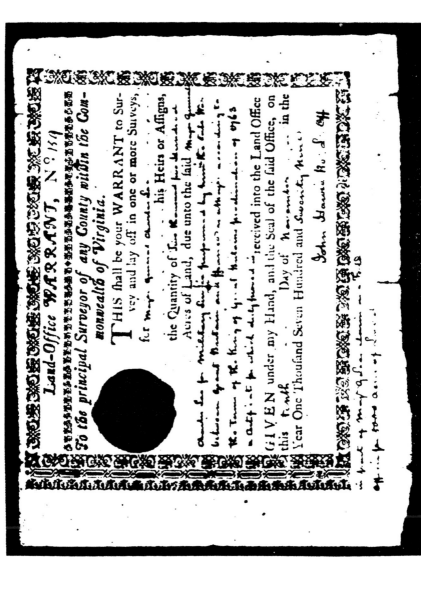

Land-Office WARRANT, N.º 159

To the principal Surveyor of any County within the Commonwealth of Virginia.

THIS shall be your WARRANT to Survey and lay off in one or more Surveys, for _____ _____ _____ his Heirs or Assigns,

the Quantity of _____ _____ _____ Acres of Land, due unto the said _____ _____

_____ _____ _____ _____ _____ _____ _____ _____ _____ _____ _____ _____ _____ 1763

GIVEN under my Hand, and the Seal of the said Land Office, on this _____ Day of November _____ in the Year One Thousand Seven Hundred and Seventy Nine.

John Harvie R. L. Off.

This is to certify that Mr James Shaw has full power
if you act in my name in anything respecting [Esau?]; that I [am]
contented and I ratify the last June[?] I made & [as] by this present.

Charles Lee

Burley County April 3[?] & 1799
John L. Thomas Esq

James [Hearns?]
Robert [Lewis?]
Thomas [Hook?]
[signatures]

Surveyed for James Town & Charles
Lee 1000 acres of land in Jefferson County
by virtue of a Military Warrant No 789
Entered April 28th 1786 on the N.W. branch
of the S. fork of Harrods Creek including
a spring & Beech Tree marked I H above
of Standing Stone Creek. Beginning
at three Iron & Beeches about 9 in. S. 1 w.
& above 120 ft nearly a N.W. course from
said spring and running N. 45 E.
355 ft to two Sugar Trees & Beech
thence S. 45 E. 450 ft to a hickory
W. Oak & Dog Wood thence N. 45 W.
355 ft to two White & Walnut
Standing on a flat thence N. 45 E. 450 ft to the Beginning.
Also 1500 acres part of the same Warrant Beginning at two Ashes
and Walnut South Corner to his 1000 acre Survey and running
S. 45 W. 958 ft to a Sugar Tree poplar & Black Oak thence Standing
on the Soft Bank of a small Bra. thence N. 45 W. 610 ft to a
large Sugar Tree and Beech crossg a Bra at 200 ft Standg Stone
Creek at 520 ft thence N. 45 E. 212 ft to two Sugar Trees and
Ash thence S. 45 E. 160 ft to a Sugar Tree Elm & Beech on the
N.W. side of a hill at 20 from the S.W. side of Standg Stone Creek
thence N. 45 E. 945 ft crossg Standg Stone to the Beginning.
Variation.   Exd & D. S. J. C.
Jno Bellon 9.6.6.   Decm 26th 1783
Matthew Busby   Geo May S.J.C.
Geo. Neale marker.

Alex.d White

Platt. 2500 Acres

Harrods Creek

E.d

Recorded

At 25.th Dec.r 1784

Rec.d B4

B P 237

Alexander White

two Surveys one of 1000 ac.
& the other of 1500

Jefferson County

Rec.d 25 Dec.mr 1784

Grant 14.th 16 Dec.mr
1785

Recorded page
(6)

Two Surveys

Saml. Thomas for to Survey to
the Wm of the Survey of different
Survey 25.th of 84

W.m White

Bundles 71-72.

No. Warrant,	Name	Rank	Acres Surveyed	
159,	Major General Charles Lee,	Major [5000],	2500,	Dec. 26, 1783, By I. Hite, Jefferson Co., on the n. branches of south fork of Harrod's Creek. Ass'd to James Nourse. [Lee's Autograph Assignment.]
762,	John Wheeler,	Soldier,	50,	Oct. 28, 1783, By Daniel Boone, Lincoln Co., on s. s. Kentucky River—in first large bottom 2 miles above mouth of "Drounding" Creek.
197,	Col. William Peachy,	Paymaster,	1000,	Mar. 13, 1784, By Robert Johnson, Fayette Co, bank of the Ohio, 17 poles above mouth of Dry Creek. [Total 5000 A.]
198,	Col. William Peachy,	Paymaster,	1000,	
703,	Col. William Peachy,	Captain,	3000,	
588,	Philip Corby,	Soldier Phillip's Co.	50,	May 20, 1784, By Isaac Cox, Jefferson County, on Froman's Creek, a branch of Beech Fork—Adj. Paul Froman—both Ass'd to James Overton.
716,	Zaccheus Corby,	Soldier Phillip's Co.	50,	
	Capt. Audley Paull,		2000,	July 20, 1774, By Jno. Floyd, Fincastle Co., on n. fork of Bear Grass Creek, a n. branch of **Kentucky** River, and about 18 miles from the same, being on the s. s. of the Ohio, and about 90 miles from the mouth of the Kentucky River—cor. to John Floyd's land—cor. to William Christian's land.
840,	Loftus Pullen,	Soldier,	50,	Jan. 12, 1785, By John Bryant, Lincoln Co., on Paint Lick Creek.

Bundle 73.

No. Warrant,	Name	Rank	Acres Surveyed	
868,	John Hay,	Soldier,	50,	Dec. 11, 1783, By Isaac Cox, Jefferson Co., on n. s. Salt River, at mouth of Plumb Creek. Ass'd to Israel Christian.
869,	Thomas Miller,	Soldier,	50,	
776,	George McCormick,	Subaltern [2000],	1000,	June 26, 1784, By John Constant, Fayette Co., on Creek that emptys into Licking between Upper and Lower Blue Licks on n. s. As'sd to Philip Pendleton—James McCallister—John Constant.

No. Warrant.	Name	Rank	Acres	Surveyed	
	Bundle 75-A.				
894,	John Anthony,	Captain,	3000,	Mar. 31, 1784,	By Christopher Irvine—Lincoln Co., on waters of Silver Creek—cor. Christopher Irvine—Samuel Bell's survey—cross Elk Garden Creek—Hugh Ross's line—John Anderson's survey.
1177,	Edward Sprigg, dec'd,	Capt. Washington's R. [3000],	1000,	Sept. 30, 1783,	By Philip Philips, Jefferson Co., cor. Shepherd Gunn, about 1 mile s. from main Forks of s. Fork of Nole Linn. Ass'd to Daniel Brodhead.
	Bundle 76.				
363,	George Muse,	Field Officer [part.]	300,	Mar. 24, 1784,	By Alex'r Breckenridge, Jefferson Co., on head waters of Little Kentucky, adj. This survey was for 1,300 acres, the 1,000 acres being on 2 Treasury Warrants issued to (Commodore) Richard Taylor, and assigned by Edmund Taylor. [George Muse was a British Officer, and, according to Gen'l James Taylor, of Newport, Ky., taught tactics to Gen'l George Washington. P. F. T.]
	Bundle 77.				
	Hon. William Byrd,	Col. of the Va. Regt.	1000,	June 3, 1774,	By James Douglas, Fincastle Co., on waters of Beargrass Creek, which falls into the Ohio at the head of the Falls—McCorkle's land—cor. to John Floyd—cor. to Southall & Charlton. [Copy of clause of Wm. Byrd's will devising to Thomas Byrd. Att. by M. Byrd. Also Certificate signed "M. Byrd."
	Bundle 79.				
990,	Samuel Miller,	Soldier Byrd's,	50,	Feb. 3, 1784,	By Thomas Montgomery, Lincoln Co., on a br. of Silver Creek, emptying at Locust Bent—William McBride's heirs. Ass'd to James Morrison.

No. Warrant	Name	Rank	Acres Surveyed	
Bundle 79.				
213,	John Coffey,	Sergeant,	200, May 1, 1785,	By Hugh Ross, Lincoln Co., on waters of Silver Creek, on a branch running in above Locust Bent, on w. fork of said Creek. Ass'd to Bazaleel Maxwell.
246,	Horatio Gates,	Field Officer,	1000, Nov. 20, 1785,	By William Lindsay, Fayette Co., on Bank Lick Creek, a branch of Licking, 1 mile above Logan's Spring. Ass'd to Samuel Meredith and George Clymer.
233,	Robert Nourse,	[3000 A],	1000, Dec. 14, 1784,	By Simon Morgan, Fayette Co., on waters of Cabbin Creek, and the n. f. of Licking —cor. John Marshall, Jr. —Ass'd to James Nourse.
Bundle 80.				
545,	Reuben Vass,	Subalt. Byrd's [part]	250, Oct. 1, 1784,	By William Hays, Fayette Co., on s. of Daniel Boone's Preemption. Ass'd by Vincent Vass, Att'y-in-fact, to William Ellis.
546,	Reuben Vass,	Subalt. Byrd's [part]	250,	
Bundle 81.				
796,	George Mercer,	Captain,	1000, July 17, 1784,	By Robert Breckenridge, Jefferson Co., cor. Israel Thompson—both Ass'd to Sam'l Beall by James Mercer, Att'y-in-fact for George Mercer, who was heir-at-law to John Fenton Mercer.
798,	John Fenton Mercer,	Ensign,	1000,	
785,	George Mercer,	Field Officer Byrd's,	1000, July 16, 1784,	By Robert Breckenridge, Jefferson Co., on Mill Creek adjoining Israel Thompson. Ass'd to Samuel Beall by James Mercer, Att'y-in-fact for George Mercer, who was heir-at-law to John Fenton Mercer.
799,	John Fenton Mercer,	Ensign Fry's,	1000,	
693,	Joseph Stevens, dec'd,	Field Officer,	2000, Dec. 10, 1783,	By Daniel Sullivan, Jefferson Co., on Gess's Fork, a branch of Brashear's Creek.—Joseph Roberts' line—Ass'd to William Heslop by Richard Stevens, heir-at-law.

No. Warrant	Name	Rank	Acres	Surveyed	
Bundle 81.					
786,	George Mercer,	Field Off. Byrd's,	1000,	May 8, 1784,	By Philip Taylor, Jefferson Co., on s. s. of a Creek running into the Ky. River, on the s. s., about 4 or 5 miles from the mouth—Mill Creek—Ass'd to Samuel Beall by James Mercer, Att'y-in-fact.
787,	George Mercer,	Field Off. Byrd's,	1000,		
791,	George Mercer,	Captain, Wash'ns,	1000,		
792,	George Mercer,	Captain, Fry's,	1000,		
802,	John Fenton Mercer,	Capt. Washington's,	1000,		
Bundle 84.					
101,	John Shingleton,	Soldier,	50,	Apr. 14, 1785,	By William Harvie, Fayette Co., on Boggs' Fork of Boon's Creek—small spring improved by Drake and John South. Ass'd to French Strother—to John Harvie.
817,	Zachary Lewis,	Subaltern Stephen's,	2000,	Apr. 8, 1781,	By W. Ward, Fayette Co., on w. s. Hickman's Trace. Ass'd to Martin Hawkins.
Bundles 85–86–87.					
	James Sullivan,		1000,	Jan. 24, 1783,	By Joseph Barnet, Jefferson Co., on n. s. Rolling Fork—mouth Price's Creek. Jacob Myers' line—Skeggs's Station.
	Jethro Sumner,		2000,	June 24, 1775,	By Jno. Floyd, Fincastle Co., on waters Elk Horn Creek.
	William Sutherland,	Ensign 95th,	1000,	June 1, 1774,	By Hancock Taylor, Fincastle Co., on Ohio River—cor. William Peachy—cor. William Bowyer.
894,	John Anthony,	[part]	318,	Apr. 9, 1785,	By Christopher Irvine, Lincoln Co., on waters Silver Creek—cor. Christopher Irvine Ass'nee Callaway—Elverton Peyton's line—Stone Lick—George Smith's line—on Taylor's Fork of Silver Creek.
415,	Edward Sutton,	Sold. 1st Va.,	50,	May 27, 1784,	By James Rentfro, Lincoln Co., on "Cantucka River,"—Paint Lick—cor. Humphrey Thompkins.
	Charles Knight,	Sergt. [War't 500]	200,		
501,	James Samuel,	Private,	50,		
364,	George Muse,	Field Off. [part].	50,	June 15, 1785,	By Richard Woolfolk, Jefferson Co., on Ohio River, about 20 miles above Falls. Both Ass'd to Richard Taylor by Hubbard Taylor, Att'y for George Muse.
366,	George Muse,	Field Off. [part].	950,		
742,	John Barksdale,	Serjeant,	100,		Ass'd to Richard Taylor.

Bundle 88.

No. Warrant.	NAME	RANK	ACRES SURVEYED	
707, 708.	Thomas Hitchcock, Newman Boulware, dec'd,	Soldier, Byrd's, Soldier,	50, 50,	Oct. 30, 1783, By Arthur Fox—Jefferson Co., on Ohio about 18 or 20 miles above Falls—cor. John Carter—No. 708 to Margaret Jennett [?] and Eliza Boulware, co-heirs. Both Ass'd to John Craig—to Elijah Craig.
705,	Augustin Ramsay,	Soldier,	50,	To Margaret, Milly and Anne Ramsay, legal reps.
706,	Richard Evans, dec'd,	Soldier,	50,	Feb. 11, 1784, To Elizabeth Evans, legal representative. By Arthur Fox, Jefferson Co., on Ohio, cor. John Carter—18 mile Creek—Ass'd to John Craig—to Elijah Craig.
548, 549,	Reuben Vass, Reuben Vass,	Subaltern, Byrd's, Subaltern, Byrd's,	500, 500,	July 23, 1784, By William Hays, Fayette Co., on waters of Licking—Enoch Smith's line. Issued to Vincent Vass, Att'y. Ass'd to John Chiles.
193,	Archibald Thompson,		200,	Dec. 22, 1783, By Septimus Davis, Fayette Co.—cor. Chapman Austin—Ass'd to Israel Christian.
106, 112,	Dominick Mourning, William Camp,	Sold. 1st Va., Corporal Washington's,	50, 200,	Oct. 10, 1783, By Ben. Patton, Fayette Co., on waters of Jessamine Creek. Joins Adam Stephen.
469, 1388,	Francis Irvin, John Campbell,	Private, [2000],	50, 1000,	Ass'd to Joseph Craig. Dec. 22, 1783, By Daniel Sullivan. Jefferson Co., on Fox Run—John Paull's line—Jacob Myers' Preemption [1000 acres Ass'd to John Connelly, Oct. 21, 1783.]
701,	John Sallard,	Subaltern Byrd's,	2000,	Sept. 10, 1784, By Daniel Boone, Fayette Co., on creek emptying into Licking, 9 miles below lower Salt Springs, Ass'd to Lewis Craig.

Bundles 89 90.

No. Warrant.	NAME	RANK	ACRES SURVEYED	
223,	Benjamin Winslow,	Subaltern,	500,	Ass'd to Daniel Boone (but Plat and survey has been removed from file).

No. Warrant.	Name	Rank	Acres Surveyed	
	Bundle 91.			
564,	David Stewart.	Commissarye Col. Andrew Lewis's Expedition against the Indians.	2000, Nov. 1, 1784,	By Richard Woolfolk, Jefferson Co., on Little Ky.— cor. Smith and Preston's line. To John Stewart, son and heir.
		Bundle 93.		
100,	Henry Brown,	Soldier Byrd's,	50, Dec. 7, 1784,	By Ben. Patton, Fayette Co., on waters of Bowman's Creek.
464,	James Twopence,	Soldier Christian's Rangers,	50,	
		Bundle 94.		
	James Buford,	Serjeant,	200, Aug. 5, 1775,	By John Floyd, Fincastle Co., near the head of Middle Fork of Elk Horn—joins John Maxwell—Ass'd to James Cowden—to Charles Cummins—to John Floyd.
	William Christian,	Capt. Va. Regt.,	1000, June 12, 1774,	By James Douglass, Fincastle Co., on Salt River, about 20 miles from the Falls, including the Salt Springs and Buffaloe Lick.
	Arthur Campbell,		1000, June 3, 1774,	By Jno. Floyd, Fincastle Co., on branches of Bear Grass Creek, about a mile from same—cor. Harrison—John Connelly's line.
	John Allen, dec'd,		2000, June 22, 1776,	By Jno. Floyd, Fincastle Co., on waters of Salt River. To James Allen, representative.
	William Inglis,	Lieut, [2,000],	1000, July 18, 1774,	By Jno. Floyd, Fincastle Co., on waters of Elk Horn, on s. s. thereof, about 20 miles from Ky. River—John Draper's line.
	John Ware,	Capt. [3000 A] part.	1000, July 15, 1774,	By Jno. Floyd, Fincastle Co., on n. branches of Ky. River, about 5 miles e. of the head of Elk Horn Creek—cor. to Samuel Meredith—Ass'd to Patrick Henry—by him [Autograph] to Thomas Madison.

I do hereby certify that Griffin Peart is intitled as Ensign in the Virginia Regiment under the Command of Colo Washington to two thousand Acres of Land Agreeable to his Majesty's Proclamation of October 1763 and being desirous of locating the same on some of the Western Waters, You are hereby strictly Authorized and Required to Survey the same two thousand Acres whereso ever the said Griffin Peart shall require it, taking care not to interfere with any Surveys which hath been made by Order of Council or Patents already Granted, and this shall be your Warrant for so doing

Given under my hand and Seal
this 17th day of December 1773

To The Surveyer
of Fincastle County

Sir
Mr Hancock Taylor is hereby empowered
to Direct my Survey or Surveys

To Colo William Preston

Dunmore

Griffin Peart

Bundle 94.

No. Warrant,	Name	Rank	Acres Surveyed	
	Griffin Peart,	Ensign Washingt'n,	2000, June 30, 1774,	By Hancock Taylor, Fincastle Co., on Elk Horn—cor. to Charles Lewis—Autograph certificate of Lord Dunmore as to service. Dec. 17, 1773. [See this.]
	William Peachy,	Field Officer,	2000, Aug. 4, 1778,	By Jno. Floyd, Fincastle Co., in the fork at the junction of the Ohio and Ky. Rivers, on east side of Ky., cor. to William Christian.
	Thomas Dean,	Serjeant,	200, May 11, 1774,	By Jno. Floyd, Fincastle Co., on s. s. Ohio R., in first large bottom about 9 miles above Big Miami—cor. Hugh Mercer.
	William Peachy,	Field Off. 2d Va.,	2000, July 7, 1774,	By Hancock Taylor, Fincastle Co., on Elk Horn—cor. Philip Love.
	John Hickman,	Lieutenant,	1000, July 13, 1774,	By James Douglas, Fincastle Co., n. s. of Ky. R., John Willis and Jacob Sadusky, Chain Carriers.
	Thomas Gist,		2000, June , 1775,	By James Douglas, Fincastle Co., on Gist's Creek.
	Christopher Gist,		3000, June , 1775,	By James Douglas, Fincastle Co., on n. s. of Ky. River, on Gist's Creek, a br. of the Licking. Survey to Thomas Gist. "Let the Patent issue in the name of Nathaniel Gist, who is oldest son and heir-at-law of Christopher Gist (signed) Wm. Preston, S. F. C."
	William Preston,	Captain [3000],	1000, June 6, 1774,	By Jno. Floyd, Fincastle Co., on the branches of the Ohio, on s. s. of same—cor. Col. Byrd's line—McCorkle's upper cor.—1398 poles from the Falls of the Ohio, at the mouth of Bear Grass Creek.

Bundle 94.

No. Warrant	Name	Rank	Acres Surveyed	
Warrant,	Col. William Preston,	Captain [3000],	1000, Aug. 9, 1775,	By I[saac] Hite, Fincastle Co., on s. e. of Kentucky R., about 25 miles from mouth. Ass'd to Abraham Hite and Peter Hog.
	Col. William Fleming,	Captain,	3000, June 2, 1774,	By Jno. Floyd, Fincastle Co., on the Ohio 590 poles below Connelly's lower corner—about 5 miles below the Falls—cor. to Thomas Bowyer and John Ware. [Copy of Dunmore's certificate.]
	Hugh Allen,		1000, June 7, 1774,	By Jno. Floyd, Fincastle Co., on waters of Bear Grass Ck., about 5 miles from the Ohio—cor. Charleton and Southall's survey.
	John Draper,	Officer,	1000, June 6, 1774,	By Jno. Floyd, Fincastle Co., on waters Bear Grass, about 3 or 4 miles from Falls, by a Buffaloe trace crossing Creek. Ass'd to John Floyd.
	William Peachy,	Field Officer,	1000, June 1, 1774,	By Hancock Taylor, Fincastle Co., on the Ohio—cor. Hancock Eustace, about 1541 poles above mouth of Bear Grass, cor. David Robinson.
	John Bowyer,		1000, June 4, 1775,	By Jno. Floyd, Fincastle Co., on branch of Floyd's Creek, about 3 miles from Ky. River—cor. Dandridge. Ass'd to William Madison.
	John Ashby,	Capt. Co. of Rangers,	3000, June 8, 1774,	By Hancock Taylor, Fincastle Co., on head branches of Bear Grass Creek [Warrant for 3000 acres].
	Walter Stewart,	Serjeant, 44th R.,	200, July 10, 1776,	By Jno. Floyd, Fincastle Co., on a branch of Licking Creek.
	Alexander Spotswood,		2000, July 11, 1774,	By Jno. Floyd, Fincastle Co., on waters of Elk Horn Creek, about 90 miles from the Ohio—William Naskes [?] land. Issued to Alexander Spotswood Dandridge, Assignee.

No. Warrant,	Name	Rank	Acres Surveyed	
	Bundle 94.			
	John Waller,	Lieut. 2d. Va.,	1000, June 20, 1774,	By Hancock Taylor, Fincastle Co., on waters of Elk Horn Creek, Ass'd to Alexander Waugh—to Hancock Taylor—Patented to Zachary Taylor, his heir-at-law.
	John Ashby,	Capt. Rangers,	2000, June 23, 1774,	By Hancock Taylor, Fincastle Co., on n. s. Ky. R., cor. to Hancock Taylor.
	Samuel Meredith,	Captain,	2000, July 11, 1774,	By Jno. Floyd, Fincastle Co., waters of Elk Horn Creek—cor. William Christain—cor. Alexander Spotswood Dandridge.
	Alexander Spotswood,		1000, June 6, 1774,	By Jno. Floyd, Fincastle Co., on waters of Bear Grass Creek, on s. fork, 650 poles from Falls of Ohio—land surveyed for Col. William Preston, in a line of Hancock Taylor, To Alexander Spotswood Dandridge, Assignee.
	James Robinson,	Subaltern [2000],	1000, July 15, 1774,	By Jno. Floyd, Fincastle Co., about 5 miles e. of the head of Elk Horn Creek, 30 miles from the Ky. R.—cor. to Thomas Hinds—To Patrick Henry, Assignee—Ass'd to Thomas Madison.
	Thomas Carter,	Ensign,	2000, July 14, 1774,	By Jno. Floyd, Fincastle Co., on branches of Elk Horn Creek—cor. to William Phillips—To John Carter, rep. of Thomas Carter, dec'd. Articles of agreement between John Carter, of City of Williamsburg, Merchant, and Elijah Craig, of Orange, July 26, 1779.
	John Hickman,		1000, July 13, 1774,	By James Douglas, Fincastle Co., on n. s. Ky. R.—cor. to Hon. William Byrd—cor. Capt. Robert McKensie.
	John Ware,	[3000],	1000, July 9, 1774,	By Jno. Floyd, Fincastle Co., on brs. of Elk Horn Creek—cor. Col. Christian. Ass'd to Richard Cave.

Bundle 94.

No. Warrant,	NAME	RANK	ACRES SURVEYED	
	William Hugart,	Lieutenant,	1000, June 14, 1775,	By Jno. Floyd, Fincastle Co., on Licking Creek, to Thomas Hugart, Ass'd to Thomas Wright.
	John Lawson,	Lieut., 2d Va.,[2000],	1000, May 26, 1774,	By Hancock Taylor, Fincastle Co., on the Ohio, about 16 miles below mouth of Ky. R.—John Lawson, of Fauquier; Ass'd to Martin Pickett of Fauquier, July 12, 1779.
	Thomas Hickman,		2000,	By Jno. Floyd, Fincastle Co., on brs. of Boon's Creek, which runs into Ky. about 4 miles below Boonesborough. To James Hickman, rep.
	John Ware,	[3000],	1000, July 9, 1774,	By Jno. Floyd, Fincastle Co., on brs. of Elk Horn Creek—cor. Col. Christian—Ass'd to Richard Cave.
	William Hugart,	Lieutenant,	1000, June 14, 1775,	By Jno. Floyd, Fincastle Co., on Licking Creek; to Thomas Hugart, Ass'd to Thomas Wright.
	John Lawson,	Lieut. 2d Va. [2000],	1000, May 26, 1774,	By Hancock Taylor, Fincastle Co., on Ohio, about 16 miles below mouth of Ky. R. John Lawson, of Fauquier, Ass'd to Martin Pickett, of Fauquier, July 12, 1779.
	Thomas Hickman,		2000, July 18, 177-,	By Jno. Floyd, Fincastle Co., on brs. Boon's Creek; to James Hickman, rep.
	William Henry,	Lieut. [2000],	1000, July 9, 1774,	By Jno. Floyd, Fincastle Co., on waters of Elk Horn; cor. to Jno. Floyd; cor. to Patrick Henry; Ass'd to John Sutton.
	Hugh Allen, dec'd,		1000 June 25, 1776,	By John Floyd; Fincastle Co., on waters Clear Creek, a br. of the Ky., about 10 miles above Harrod's Landing; cor. Rollins; to John Allen, heir-at-law.

Bundle 94.

No. Warrant, NAME	RANK	ACRES SURVEYED	
George Elliott,		200, May 21, 1774,	By John Floyd, Fincastle Co., on Ohio, joining and below mouth of Ky., surveyed for Francis Preston and John Smith, Ass'nees of Francis Smith; Ass'nee of George Elliott.
Matthew Anderson,	Non-com.,	200, May 27, 1774,	By Jno. Floyd, Fincastle Co., on the Ohio, about 19 miles above Falls; beg. at mouth of Creek, just above 3rd island above Falls; to John Carter, Ass'd to Elijah Craig.
Henry Russell,	Subaltern,	2000, July 12, 1774,	By Jno. Floyd, Fincastle Co., on a n. branch of Ky. River, about 95 miles from the Ohio; cor. Alexander Spotswood Dandridge; to William Russell, heir-at-law.
Captain Henry Harrison, dec'd,		1000, June 7, 1774,	By Jno. Floyd, Fincastle Co., on waters of Bear Grass about 5 miles from Ohio; cor. John Ware; to Henry Harrison, son and heir.
John Blagg,	Capt. 1st Va.	[3000], 1000, June 3, 1774,	By Jno. Floyd, Fincastle Co., on Bear Grass; cor. to Alexander Waugh, Finnie and Charleton, 800 poles from the Ohio, and 1½ miles above the Falls; to James McCorkle, Ass'nee of Daniel Trigg, Ass'nee of John Blagg.
Leroy Griffin, dec'd,		2000, May 27, 1775,	By John Floyd, Fincastle Co., on Ohio, about 18 or 20 miles from Falls; 2 miles below the 3rd island above Falls; near Harrod's Creek; to Judith Griffin, daughter.
Samuel McDowell,		2000, July 11, 1775,	By Jno. Floyd, Fincastle Co., on waters of Elk Horn.

Bundle 94.

No. Warrant,	Name	Rank	Acres Surveyed	
	William Christian,		1000, May 12, 1774,	By Jno. Floyd, Fincastle Co., on a s. branch of the Ohio called Big Bone Creek, including the large Buffalo Lick and Salt Spring, being about 4 miles from the Ohio.
	James McDowell, dec'd,		1000, June 14, 1775,	By Jno. Floyd, Fincastle Co., on a s. fork of Licking Creek; to James McDowell, heir-at-law.
	Lieut. Peter Steenbergen,		2000, Nov. 8, 1775,	By I[saac] Hite, Fincastle Co., on Hickman's Creek, a branch of Kentucky R.; cor. James Douglas; to Col. Abraham Hite, Ass'nee.
	James Robinson,	Subaltern;	1000, July 16, 1774,	By Jno. Floyd, Fincastle Co., about 5 miles e. of the head branches of Elk Horn, and 32 miles from the Ky.; cor. Patrick Henry. Ass'd to Thomas Hind [Hinde?].
	Thomas Waggoner,	Capt. Washington's,	3000, July 4, 1774,	By Hancock Taylor; Fincastle Co., on s. fork of Elk Horn; cor. to Slaughter and Jones; to Andrew Waggoner, heir-at-law. Ass'd to Edmund Taylor.
	Thomas Bowyer,		1000, July 13, 1774,	By Jno. Floyd, Fincastle Co., on Elk Horn; cor. Vaughan's line.
	Jethro Sumner,		2000, June 24, 1775,	By Jno. Floyd, Fincastle Co., on waters of Elk Horn, and called "Sumner's Forest."
	Turner Southall,		2000, June 27, 1774,	By Jno. Floyd, Fincastle Co., on Elk Horn, beg. on s. bank of Creek by a large Buffaloe ford, 360 poles above Cove Run [Cave Run]; Ass'd to Bartholomew Dandridge.
	Alexander Waugh		1000. July 21, 1774,	By Jno. Floyd, Fincastle Co., on Elk Horn; Ass'd to William Preston; to John Floyd.

Bundle 94.

No. Warrant,	Name	Rank	Acres Surveyed	
	Captain Henry Harrison, dec'd,		1000, June 2, 1774,	By Jno. Floyd, Fincastle Co., on s. s. Ohio, 2¼ miles from the head of Falls; cor. Thomas Bowyer and William Fleming; to Henry Harrison, son and heir.
	John Smith,	Capt. New Levies [3000]	1000, June 29, 1775,	By Jno. Floyd, Fincastle Co., on branches Spring Creek, a br. of Ky. River; line of Glen's land; cor. to Moffett; to George Skillern, Ass'nee; ass'd to William Preston.
	William Preston,	Captain [3000],	1000, July 13, 1774,	By Jno. Floyd, Fincastle Co., on Elk Horn; cor. William Phillips' land. Ass'd Oct. 8, 1779, to Joseph Rogers and John Seabery. [SEE THIS.]
	Thomas Fleming]	Captain,	3000, July 7, 1774,	By Jno. Floyd, Fincastle Co., on Elk Horn; on draft running into s. fork—crossing n. fork. Ass'd to Patrick Henry.
	William Phillips,	Major,	3000,	Fincastle; on branches of Elk Horn. [Survey Torn.]
	John Savage,	[3000],	1000,	By Jno. Floyd, Fincastle Co., land known as Cave [or Cove] Spring; s. fork of Elk Horn. Ass'd to Abraham Hite; surveyed to William Preston.
	Nathaniel Gist,		3000, June , 1775,	By James Douglas, Fincastle Co., on n. s. Ky. R., on Gist's Creek; to Thomas Gist, representative.
	Alexander Finnie, father, William Finnie, son,	Lieut. Byrd's, Surgeon's Mate, Byrd's,	2000, 2000, June 1, 1774,	By James Douglas, Fincastle Co., on Ohio; R[ichard] Taylor's line; above mouth of Bear Grass; Ass'd to Richard Charleton and James Southall. [This
	John Finnie, son,	Ensign Byrd's,	2000,	is now the heart of Louisville.]

Bundle 95.

No. Warrant,	Name	Rank	Acres Surveyed	
63,	Benjamin Powell,	Serjeant Byrd's,	200,	Nov. 25, 1783, By Jo. Helm, Jefferson Co., on Clover Creek, Meriweather's line; Hite's Run. Ass'd to James Madison.
231,	Samuel Young,	Sergeant,	200,	Nov. 24, 1783, By Jo. Helm, Jefferson Co.. on Clover Creek, formerly called Hargises Fork; adj. Powell's survey. Ass'd to James Madison.
873,	Barney Ryley,	Soldier,	50,	[No Survey found.]

Bundles 96-97.

41,	James Hendrick,	Captain [3000],	500,	Nov. 25, 1783, By I. Hite, Jefferson Co., on waters of Town Fork of Salt R.; joins Charles Simms. To Rev. David Griffith, Ass'nee.
759,	John Hall, dec'd,	Sergt. Phillip's Co.,	200,	Nov. 23, 1783, By Daniel Boone, Fayette Co., on a small br. of Licking; adj. Daniel Boone's Settlement.
390,	Henry Cissel, dec'd, [To Wm. Cissel, heir-at-law.]	Soldier,	50,	Sept. 7, 1783, By Arch'd Campbell, Fayette Co., near head waters of Huston's Fork of Licking and Elk Horn. All Ass'd to John Hord.
391,	James Cissel, dec'd, [To Wm. Cissel, heir-at-law.]	Soldier,	50,	
392,	William Cissel,	Soldier,	50,	
393,	William Mitchell,	Soldier,	50,	
672,	Joseph Ray,	Capt. Stanwix's Com'd,	500,	Nov. 22, 1783, By James Kincaid, Lincoln Co., on Sugar Creek; Dewitt's survey. Ass'd to William Hamilton.
409,	William Hughes,	Serjeant,	200,	Nov. 24, 1783, By Daniel Boone, Fayette Co.
355,	Francis Scott,	Soldier,	50,	Mar. 13, 1784, By Joshua Bennett, Fayette Co., including the two Salt Springs at the Lower Blue Licks, on Licking Creek; to James Parberry, ass'nee of William Floyd, ass'nee of John Floyd, ass'nee of Philip Love, ass'nee of Turner H. Hudson, ass'nee of Francis Scott.

No. Warrant	Name	Rank	Acres Surveyed	
	Bundles 96–97.			
897,	David Crews,	Corporal,	200, Mar. 19, 1783,	By Jesse Cartwright, Fayette Co., on Ky. River, opposite mouth of Jack's Creek.
381,	Gabriel Throckmorton,	Captain [part],	250, Nov. 11, 1783,	By B. Netherland, Jefferson Co., on E. fork of Floyd's Fork; cor. William Bartlett; William Hoblay's line; to James Crain, ass'nce of William Bartlett, ass'nee of Gabriel Throckmorton.
86,	Thomas Buford,	Captain [part],	1000, Jan. 29, 1784,	By William Montgomery, Lincoln Co., 337 acres on head branches of Henry's Fork; Isaac Shelby's line; cor. to George Givens; Owen Davers' line; to Samuel Craig, Ass'nce.
49,	Thomas Barron,	Serjeant,	200,	[No Survey]. Ass'd to Abraham Hite.
	Bundle 98.			
	George Elliott, [Certificate signed Jan. 27, 1774, by Dunmore.]		200, May 6, 1774,	By Jno. Floyd. Fincastle Co., on Ohio, 49 miles below mouth of Scioto; to John Smith, Ass'nce.
	James Buford, [Certificate signed Apr. 19, 1774, by Dunmore.]	Sarjent,	200.	
389,	Butor[?] Buckley,	Soldier,	50, June 11, 1784,	By Thomas Lillard, Lincoln Co., on Rowling Fork, about 6 miles from Carpenter's Sta. Ass'd to James Speed.
82,	Evan Shelby,	Major [part],	500, Aug. 13, 1784,	By Arthur Fox, Fayette Co., joins Isaac Shelby—Patrick Henry's line.
129,	Charles Tomkies,	Subaltern,	500, May 15, 1784,	By Arthur Fox, Fayette Co., on head-waters Green Creek; cor. Thomas Hind's [Hindess]; John Rogers' survey. Ass'd to Isaac Shelby.
768,	William Hughes,	Subaltern,	2000, Nov. 23, 1783,	By Daniel Boone, Fayette Co., about 2 miles e. of William Cork's Cabin.

No. Warrant,	Name	Rank	Acres	Surveyed	
	Bundle 98.				
513,	Nathaniel Gist,	Captain,	3000,	Sept. 26, 1783,	By Benjamin Field, Jefferson Co., on Panther Creek. Ass'd to John Smith.
514,	Nathaniel Gist,	Captain,	3000,		To Nathaniel Gist, son and heir; ass'd to John Smith.
515,	Nathaniel Gist,	Captain,	3000,		
516,	Christopher Gist,	Captain,	3000,		
	Bundle 99.				
591,	Charles Barrett,	Serg't Phillips' Co.,	200,	Mar. 23, 1784,	By Waller Overton, Fayette Co., on Clear Creek; joins James Bullock.
384,	Gabriel Throckmorton,	Captain [part],	250,	Nov. 8, 1783,	By B. Netherland, Jefferson Co., on waters of e. fork of Floyd's Fork; cor. William Hobday. To William Bartlett, Ass'nee.
385,	Gabriel Throckmorton,	Captain [part],	250,		
386,	Gabriel Throckmorton,	Captain [part],	250,		
1320,	Philip Barbour,	Capt., Steven's Л.,	3000,	Apr. 15, 1784,	By Richard Barbour, Jefferson Co., on the Ohio about ½ mile below the edge of the Plains.
743,	John Barksdale,	Serg't 1st Va.,	100,	Nov. 10, 1783,	By B. Netherland, Jefferson Co., on waters of e. fork of Floyd's Fork; cor. Francis Tate.
1316,	Jacob Kelly,	Soldier,	50,	Dec. 27, 1782,	By William Henry, Lincoln Co., cor. to Caldwell; to Robert Brumfield, Ass'nee.
1317,	Joseph Hurt,	Soldier,			
290,	John Hamilton,	Subaltern,	1000,	Jan. 21, 1783,	By Samuel Grant, Fayette Co., on waters of Stoner's Fork of Licking; cor. Thomas Montague; cor. Lewis and Elijah Craig; cor. William Ellis. Ass'd to James Black by Andrew Hamilton, assignee of John Hamilton.
589,	James Bullock,	Subaltern Phillips' Co.,	2000,	Mar. 22, 1784,	By Waller Overton, Fayette Co., on Kentucky River and Clear Creek.
	Bundle 100.				
1148,	William Blanton,	Serjeant,	200,	Feb. 14, 1785,	By Christopher Irvine, Lincoln Co., on waters of Taylor's Fork of Silver Creek; adj. William Cowan; Sherley's Lick Fork.

Bundle 101.

No. Warrant	Name	Rank	Acres	Surveyed	
924, 927,	Francis Smith, John Norris,	Lieutenant, Soldier,	2000, 50,	Jan. 19, 1783,	By Alex'r Breckenridge, Jefferson Co., on head branches of a creek between Floyd's Fork and Bullskin; cor. Alex'r Breckenridge; cor. William Preston, jun'r.
770,	John Clark,	Sergeant,	200,	Nov. 27, 1783,	By J. Crawford, Jefferson Co., on Green River; to Andrew Reid, ass'nee of Samuel McDowell, ass'nee of John Clark.
279,	Edward Blackburn,	Subaltern,	500,	Mar. 22, 1784,	By Green Clay, Lincoln Co., on Ky. R., about 1 mile below mouth of Drowning Creek; to James Reid, Ass'nee of George Blackburn, heir-at-law of Edward Blackburn.
183,	John Buford,		200,	Oct. 8, 1783,	By Samuel Grant, Lincoln Co., on e. s. Dick's R., John Buford, heir-at-law, assigns to Robert Scott.
205, 919,	James Robertson, James Robertson,	Sejeant, Subaltern,	200, 2000,	Jan. 21, 1783,	By Alex'r Breckenridge, Jefferson Co., on a creek between Floyd's Fork and Bullskin; cor. James Kemp; cor. Samuel Beall.

Bundle 102.

No. Warrant	Name	Rank	Acres	Surveyed	
299,	William Hughes,	Adj't Washington's,	2000,	Mar. 16, 1784,	By Daniel Sullivan, Jefferson Co., waters of Gesses Creek, a branch of Brushear's Creek; adj. Samuel Beall; to John May, ass'nee.
302.	Abner Nash,	Lieutenant,	500,	No Survey;	Ass'd to John May.

Bundle 103-A.

No. Warrant	Name	Rank	Acres	Surveyed	
	William Bradley,	Ensign.	2000,	July 17, 1774,	By Jno. Floyd, Fincastle Co., 1000 acres on waters of Elk Horn, about 20 miles from Ky. River; cor. Thomas Barnes and William Christian; William Phillips' line; Ass'd to William Christian; to Adam Smith; to Isaac Hite, et al.

No. Warrant,	Name	Rank	Acres	Surveyed
Bundle 103-A.				
134	Moses Collier,	Soldier Byrd's,	50,	Apr. 7, 1784, By Hugh Ross, Lincoln Co., on main Silver Creek; including an old Indian town, house and spring; Round Hill bottom; Ass'd to William Whitley; to John Kennedy and to his heirs by copy of will attached.
761.	John Freeman,	Soldier Phillips' Co.,	50,	Ass'd to John Atkins; No Survey.
Bundle 103-B.				
	Hancock Eustace,	Captain,	1000,	June 1, 1774, By Hancock Taylor, Fincastle Co., on the Ohio, about 3 miles above the Falls; cor. Hugh Mercer; cor. William Peachy; Copy of Will dated May 28, 1766; probated Northumberland Co., Oct. 9, 1775, devising to wife, Isabella; Copy of Will of Isabella Eustace, date May 15, 1778; probated Williamsburg Nov. 6, 1779; devising to Nancy Eustace, reputed daughter of my said late husband; and to my cousin, John Blair; certificate, July 22, 1785, of Joseph and Samuel Blackwell, that Nancy Eustace married in 1780 to William Jones.
601.	William Dangerfield,	Capt. Stephen's, [3000 A.],	2000,	Apr. 30, 1784, By W. Clarke, Jefferson Co., on upper side of mouth of Salt River; run up the Ohio; cross a fork of Pond Creek; to Benjamin Johnston, assignee to William Johnston.
51.	Thomas Simonds,	Soldier,	50,	Dec. 15, 1783, By I. Hite, Jefferson Co., on Goose Creek; joins Col. Christian, Col. Fleming and Abraham Hite, Sr., lines; also Edmund Taylor.

NO. Warrant.	NAME	RANK	ACRES SURVEYED	
Bundle 104.				
662	John McClanahan, dec'd,	Subaltern,	1000, Jan. 17, 1784,	By Will. Shannon, Jefferson Co., on waters of Bullskin Creek; adjoin Roger Tapp. To John McClanahan, heir-at-law; Ass'd to Robert McClenachan; to Archer Matthews; to Ann Matthews and Sarah McClenachan Matthews.
1389.	William Murray,		2000, Apr. 15, 1784,	By Daniel Sullivan, Jefferson Co., on waters of Fox Run; cor. John Paul; cor. John Campbel.
347.	John Murray, dec'd,		2000, Dec. 17, 1783,	By Daniel Sullivan, Jefferson Co., on waters of Clear Creek; cor. to Holman; Gesses Fork; to Elizabeth Murray, widow and heiress.
Bundle 108.				
141	William Dervis,	Soldier,	50, Aug. 23, 1784,	By William Mays, Fayette Co. between Ky River and Hickman's Creek; to Edward Dervis, heir-at-law; ass'd to John Fox; to Isaac Shelby; to James Shelby.
Bundle 109.				
876	Samuel Meredith,	Captain,	1000, Dec. 7, 1784,	By Isaac Cox, Jefferson Co., on n. s. Rolling Fork, at the mouth of Beech Fork.
Bundle 112.				
865, 866,	Edward Brown, John Powell.	Soldier, Soldier,	50, 50,	Nov. 14, 1783, By Andrew Steele, Fayette Co., on n. s. Ky River at mouth of Shoemakers Creek; Ass'd to Edward Brown and James Sutton.

No. Warrant.	Name	Acres Surveyed	Rank	
	Bundle 113.			
72.	John Seayres. [?]	2000, May 12, 1784,		By John Helm, Jefferson; on s. s. Sinking Creek, where Hardin's Trace crosses same; to Andrew Woodrow, administrator, with will annexed of Alexander Woodrow, dec'd, who was ass'nee of John Seayres; 500 acres ass'd to Andrew Hynes.
	Bundle 114.			
236.	Jeffrey Murrell,	50, Mar. 16, 1785,	Soldier,	By James Breckinridge, Jefferson Co., on s. fork Beargrass; Preston's line; Byrd's line; both ass'd to William Preston.
646.	Charles Howell,	50, Mar. 15, 1784,	Soldier Byrd's,	By William Roberts, Jefferson Co., on Brashear's Creek, about 3 miles from mouth; Ass'd to James Patton.
532. 533. 534.	William Cave, Richard Lamb, John Lamb,	50, 50, 50, Dec. 1, 1784,	Private Byrd's, Private Byrd's, Private Byrd's,	By Ben Patton, Fayette Co., on waters of Steven's Creek, a branch of Hinkston's Fork, adj. Ebenezer Severns; Ass'd to William Pannell.
	Bundle 115.			
194.	William Russell,	3000, Jan. 6, 1785,	Captain,	By Philip Philips, Jefferson Co., on middle fork Indian Cump Creek, about 9 miles below mouth of Big Barren; Walker Daniel's line.
407.	James McGehee,	50, Dec. 12, 1784,	Soldier,	By James Rentfro, Lincoln Co., on Tate's Creek; Ass'd to William Smith; to John Rodes.
	Bundle 116.			
	Thomas Barnes,	2000, July 13, 1774,	Qr. Mr. Sargt Va. Regt.,	By Jno. Floyd, Fincastle Co., on waters of Elk Horn and on s. s. of same, about 35 miles from Ky. River; cor. Andrew Boyd; William Phillips' line; Certificate of service signed by Lord Dunmore.
17.	William Hughes,	2000, Mar. 16, 1784,	Lieut. 1st Va.,	By Dan'l Sullivan, Jefferson Co., on waters of Gesses Creek; adjoin William Staford. Ass'd to Samuel Beall.

No. Warrant.	Name	Rank	Acres Surveyed
Bundle 117.			
600.	Mordica Buckner,	Capt. Stephen's,	3000, Mar. 1, 1785, By B. Grayson, Fayette Co., on Johnston's fork of Licking and Main Licking; Ass'd to Benjamin Johnston.
72.	Andrew Woodrow,	[part],	900, Nov. 29, 1784, By Andrew Hynes, Jefferson Co., on Shante Creek, a s. branch of Rough Creek; Ass'd to Abraham Hite and Andrew Hines.
Bundle 118.			
294.	Philip Breedlove,	Soldier,	50, Apr. 23, 1784, By Isaac Cox, Jefferson Co., on dividing flat, between Salt R., and E. Fork of Cox's Creek; about 4 miles from Simpson's Creek,
Bundle 122.			
1203.	Abraham Hite,	Deputy Qr. Mr.	2000, Oct. 27, 1784, By I. Hite, Lincoln Co., adj. Isaac Hite's pre-emption as ass'nee of Samuel Adams; north fork of Hardin's Lick.
449.	William Gibson,	Soldier, Byrd's,	50,
461.	Thomas Smith,	Soldier,	50,
718.	James Cooper,	Sold., Chas. Scott's Co. [Ass'd to Francis W. Lea.]	50, Aug. 12, 1784, By Richard Young, Fayette Co., on Jessamine Creek; Jessamine Spring branch; Lewis Craig's line. All Ass'd to Lewis Craig.
Bundle 123-124.			
729.	Robert Breckinridge, dec'd,	Capt. [Lewis' Command.]	3000, Apr. 18, 1785, By Richard Woolfolk, Jefferson Co., on Guesses Creek, a br. of Brashear's Creek; cor. William Madison; cor. Samuel Goodman. To Alexander Breckinridge, heir-at-law.
542.	William Phillips,	Soldier Byrd's,	50, July 1, 1784, By Christopher Irvine, Lincoln Co., on r. h. fork of Tate's Creek; cor. Ben. Quinn; crossing a br. of Silver Creek; Ass'd to Abraham Wilson; to James Quinn.

Bundles 125–128.

No. Warrant	Name	Rank	Acres Surveyed		
297.	William Hughes,	Subaltern Wash'ns,	2000,	Nov. 9, 1785,	By Richard Woolfolk, Nelson Co., on Ohio, on the Round Bottom or Big Bend; first island below Salt River, ass'd to John May.
298.	William Hughes,	Adj. Byrd's,	2000,		
304.	Abner Nash.	Lieut.	500,		
626.	David Kennedy,	Qr. Mr. Wash'n's,	1000,	Jan. 26, 1786,	By Richard Woolfolk, Nelson Co., cor. Samuel Beall, mouth of fourth creek running into Ohio, above mouth of Green River.
627.	David Kennedy,	Qr. Mr. Wash'n's,	1000,		
628.	David Kennedy,	Q. Mr. Wash'n's	1000,		
734.	Adam Stephen,	Captain,	3000,		
244.	Horatio Gates,	Field Officer,	1000,	Nov. 16, 1785,	By William Lindsay, Fayette Co., on main fork of Creek running into the Ohio 2½ or 3 miles above mouth of Big Bone Creek.
245.	Horatio Gates,	Field Officer,	1000,		

Bundles 127–128.

No. Warrant	Name	Rank	Acres Surveyed		
109.	Joseph Hawkins,	Soldier,	50,	Oct. 31. 1785,	By William Hays, Fayette Co., on waters of Bogges Fork; cor. Madison; cor. Logan. Ass'd to Benjamin Craig; to Richard Graves.
109.	Elijah Hawkins,	Soldier,	50,		
269.	Daniel McClelland,	Soldier,	50,	Nov. 1, 1785,	By William Hays; Fayette Co., on waters of Boges Fork; cor. Logan; Ass'd to Banjamin Craig; to Richard Graves.
437.	Joseph Parrish,	Serj't 2d Va.,	200,		

Bundle 129.

No. Warrant	Name	Rank	Acres Surveyed		
632.	David Kennady,	Qr. Mr. Capt. Stew-art's [Troop of Horse.]	1000,	Nov. 10, 1785,	By John Helm, Nelson Co., on Ohio, first Island below mouth of Salt R. Ass'd to John May.
633.	David Kennady,	Qr. Mr. Capt. Stew-art's [Troop of Horse.]	1000,		
733.	Adam Stephen.	Field Off. Wash'n's,	5000,	Jan. 4, 1786,	By John Helm, Nelson Co., on Ohio, about 28 miles above mouth of Green River; cor. George Mason; first Creek above Yellow Banks; Ass'd to John May.
738.	Gabriel Throckmorton,	Capt. Peachy's,	3000,		
732.	Adam Stephen,	Field Off., Byrd's,	5000,		
736.	Gabriel Throckmorton,	Field Off. Fry's,	5000,		
739.	Gabriel Throckmorton,	Sub. Byrd's,	2000,		
629.	David Kennady,	Sub., Washington's,	1000.		

No. Warrant,	Name	Rank	Acres Surveyed	
	Bundle 129.			
630.	David Kennady,	Qr. Mr. Stephen's,	1000,	
631.	David Kennady,	Qr. Mr. Stephen's,	1000,	
821.	Julius Webb,	Sold., Throckmorton's,	50,	May 13, 1784, By John Handley, Nelson Co., on Otter Creek; including May's mill seat.
	Bundles 130–132.			
211.	Fisher Barnett,	Soldier,	50,	Aug. 8, 1785, By A. Venable, Fayette Co., opposite mouth of Silver Creek.
	Col. William Byrd,	Colonel [part],	1000,	No date, Certified by William Preston, Jefferson Co., on Bear Grass; cor. McCorkle and Floyd; cor. Southall and Charleton; to Thomas Taylor Byrd, legatee; letters, etc., of M[ary] Byrd, Ex'x, attached.
92.	David Kennady,		200,	Sept. 14, 1785—By Will. Oldham, Deputy to Alex'r Breckenridge, S. J. C.,Jefferson Co., on Mann's Lick, about 12 miles s. w. of Falls; Ass'd to Bryan Brinn[?]; to Charles Minn Thruston; to Col. John Todd, date, Falls of Ohio, Mar. 23, 1780; wit. Edmund Taylor.
	Bundle 133.			
635.	Reuben Vass,	Subaltern Stephen's,	2000,	Feb. 15, 1785, By Samuel Grant; Fayette Co., adj. John Grant's Settlement; cor. Wm. Grant; cor. Lilly; Ass'd by Vincent Vass, att'y to Thomas Montague.
608.	John Summers,	Serjeant, Byrd's,	200,	Sept. 23, 1783, By Daniel Sullivan, Jefferson Co., on Floyd's Fork; cor. McCarty; Ass'd to George Rogers Clarke.
	John Paulson,		1000,	July 13, 1774, By James Douglas, Fincastle Co., on n. s. Ky. R., waters of Jessamine Creek; cor. to Stephen; Copy of record given Col. John Montgomery, at request of Col. John Todd, Escheator of Fayette Co. [See Bundle 155.]

Bundles 136–137.

No. Warrant.	Name	Rank	Acres Surveyed	
874.	Nicholas Brabston.		200, Dec. 28, 1785,	By W. Barnet, Nelson Co., on w. fork of Pitman's Creek; ass'd to John Edmiston; to Moses Kirkpatrick.

Bundles 138–140.

No. Warrant.	Name	Rank	Acres Surveyed	
155.	John Furnace [To John Furnace, heir-at-law.]	Sold., Hogg's Com.,	50, Nov. 1, 1785,	By Richard Woolfolk, Nelson Co., on Ohio, below mouth Salt River, Abraham's Run; both Ass'd to Elijah Craig; to James Barbour.
187.	Jacob Crosthwait.	Sold. Byrd's,	50,	By John Helm, Nelson Co., on Ohio, 5 or 6 miles below mouth of Clover Creek; to James Mercer, att'y-in-fact; Ass'd to Samuel Beall.
788.	George Mercer,	Field Off. Byrd's,	1000, Dec. 21, 1785,	
789.	George Mercer,	Capt. Washington's,	1000,	
795.	George Mercer,	Capt. Indep'nt Co.,	1000,	
797.	George Mercer,	Capt. Indep'nt Co.,	1000, Dec. 23, 1785,	By Richard Woolfolk, Ass't to Will May; Surveyor Nelson Co., on waters of Ohio; cor. Robert Morris, at 4th creek above Green River; cor. John May; James Mercer. Att'y cor. George Mercer, who was heir-at-law to John Fenton Mercer; Ass'd to Samuel Beall.
803.	John Fenton Mercer.	Capt. Washington's,	1000,	
804.	John Fenton Mercer,	Capt. Washington's,	1000,	
800.	John Fenton Mercer.	Lieut. Ind. Co. of Horse Com'd by Col. Robert Stewart,	1000, Jan. 3, 1786,	By John Helm, Nelson Co., on large br. of Ohio, 8 miles above Green R., cor. George Mason; Ass'd to Samuel Beall, by James Mercer, att'y-in-fact for George Mercer, who was heir-at-law to John Fenton Mercer.
801.	John Fenton Mercer,		1000,	

Bundles 141–142–143.

No. Warrant.	Name	Rank	Acres Surveyed	
343.	John Clarke.	Serjeant,	200, Feb. 21, 1785,	By W. Ward, Fayette Co., cor. to John Ramsay; Ass'd to Elijah Richards; to Josiah Richards.
457.	Richard Riddle,	Soldier,	50, Oct. 10, 1784,	By Richard Young, Fayette Co., on waters of n. Elk Horn, on the Sink Hole Ground; cor. to John Spindler.

Bundles 141-142-143.

No. Warrant.	Name	Rank	Acres Surveyed	
516.	James Mercer.	Field Off. [2000],	1000, Dec. 24, 1785,	By Robert Todd, Fayette Co., on the Ohio, 40 poles above the first branch below mouth of Licking; down river.
			1000, Dec. 26, 1785,	By Robert Todd, Fayette Co., on the Ohio, at mouth of Big Bone Lick Creek. To John Fenton Mercer, heir to John Mercer, who was heir to James Mercer; Ass'd to Samuel Beall.

Bundles 144-145.

No. Warrant.	Name	Rank	Acres Surveyed	
521.	Anthony Kenty,	Soldier,	50, Apr. 19, 1785,	By Thomas Allen, Fayette Co., near Ohio; 4 or 5 miles above mouth of Little Mimee; cor. David Thompson; cor. Isham Prewit; to Isaac Ware, ass'nee of Anthony Kenty, who was heir-at-law to Miles Kenty, dec'd.
675.	Miles Kenty,	Sergt. John Posey's Co.,	200,	
145.	William Morris,		2000, Dec. 17, 1785,	By J. F. Moore, Jefferson Co., on Mulberry Creek, a branch of Brashear's Creek [2 surveys].
367.	George Muse,	Field Off. [part],	200, May 7, 1785,	By Robert Todd, Fayette Co., on the point of land lying between the Ohio and Licking, on the lower side; down the Ohio; Ass'd to James Taylor; to Stephen Trigg; to John Todd, Jr.

Bundles 146-147.

No. Warrant.	Name	Rank	Acres Surveyed	
256.	John Patmore,	Soldier,	50, Apr. 8, 1786,	By Will Buckner, Lincoln Co., adjoin John Hoomes; all Ass'd to Robert Rutherford; to James Crutcher.
257.	Timothy Conway,	Soldier,	50,	
258.	John Williams,	Soldier,	50,	

Bundles 148-149.

No. Warrant.	Name	Rank	Acres Surveyed	
577.	Thos. Cooper, dec'd,	Soldier, Byrd's,	50, July 15, 1785,	By Thos. Allin, Lincoln Co., on Hanging Fork of Dick's R., cor. William Cragg; cor. John Patterson; to James O'Neal, ass'nee of James Cooper, heir-at-law of Thomas Cooper, dec'd; ass'd to James Logan; to Hugh Shield.

No. Warrant,	Name	Rank	Acres Surveyed	

Bundle 152.

1192.	Arch'd Alexander,	Capt. of Co. of Vols., in an Exp. against the Shawnese Ind., [3000],	2000, Mar. 19, 1785,	By Arthur Fox, Fayette Co., on n. s. of n. fork of Licking; cor. Samuel Henry.
			1000 Mar. 20, 1785,	By Arthur Fox; adjoining other survey.
980.	Roger Corke Bailey,	Corp'l Capt. James Gunn's Co..	200, Aug. 30, 1785,	By Arthur Fox, Fayette Co., on n. s. main fork of Licking; cor. Robert Mennis; cor. John Stephenson; Ass'd to John Young.

Bundle 155.

| | John Polson | | 2000, July 13, 1776, | By James Douglas; Fincastle Co., on n. s. of Ky. River; a large spring, the head of Jessamine Creek; James Southall, cor; Adam Stephen's line; to Alexander Craig, att'y-in-fact; Autograph Certificate of Lord Dunmore; petition of Polson to House of Delegates; Report of Committee; Resolutions of House, Nov. 23, 1787. [See Bundle 133.] |

Bundles 156-157.

570.	Hon. William Byrd, dec'd,	Field. Off.,	1000, Oct. 26, 1786,	By Ro. Breckenridge, ass't to Alex'r Breckenridge, S. J. C., Jefferson Co., on the Ohio, at mouth of a creek about 12 miles above Salt River, to Mrs. Mary Byrd, Ex'x.
565.	The Hon. Wm. Byrd. dec'd,	Field Off.,	1000, Oct. 28, 1786,	By Ro. Breckenridge, Jefferson Co., on the Ohio, adjoin 1,000 acre survey; Pond Creek; To Mrs. Mary Byrd, Ex'x.
566.	The Hon. Wm. Byrd. dec'd,	Field Off..	1000,	
567.	The Hon. Wm. Byrd. dec'd,	Field Off.,	1000,	
568.	The Hon. Wm. Byrd. dec'd,	Field Off.,	1000,	
569.	The Hon. Wm. Byrd. dec'd,	Field Off.,	1000,	

Bundles 156–157.

No. Warrant	Name	Rank	Acres Surveyed	
610.	Charles Scott,	Subaltern 1st Va.,	1000,	May 27, 1785, By Jno. Waller, Fayette Co., on the Ohio;
611.	Charles Scott,	Subaltern 1st Va.,	1000,	Three Islands; mouth of Harbour Creek;
612.	Charles Scott,	Serjeant 1st Va.,	200,	Ass'd to William Finnie to Samuel
613.	Charles Scott,	Corporal 1st Va.,	200,	Beall.
614.	Charles Scott,	Soldier 1st Va.,	50,	
309.	Alex'r Finnie,	Qr. Mr. Byrd's,	400,	July 24, 1786, By John Helm, Nelson Co., on Green
310.	Alex'r Finnie,	Qr. Mr. Byrd's,	400,	River, below mouth Panther Creek, ad-
				joining Smith and Presley; to John May,
				as'nee of William Finnie, heir-at-law
				to Alexander Finnie.

Bundle 160.

No. Warrant	Name	Rank	Acres Surveyed	
624.	John Smith,	Captain,	1000,	Mar. 26, 1784, By John Fleming, Fayette Co., on Falling Timber Fork of Licking, adjoin Thomas Forbes; copy of clause of will devising to son James; Botetourt, Mar. 1783; Ass'd to Nathaniel Logan, Feb. 1, 1786; wit. D. May and Benjamin Logan.
540.	James Waldin,	Soldier Byrd's,	50,	July 7, 1784, By Christopher Irvine, Lincoln Co., on
543.	Benjamin Wheely,	Soldier Byrd's,	50,	waters Tate's Creek and Silver Creek, including ridge between, known as the Feeding Ground; cor. Benjamin Quinn; ass'd to Abraham Wilson; to John Finney [Finnie ?].

Bundle 161.

No. Warrant	Name	Rank	Acres Surveyed	
160.	Maj. Gen. Charles Lee,	Major [5000],	1000,	Aug. 18, 1783, By I. Hite, Fayette Co., on Bowman's Creek, a s. branch of Hinkston's Fork of Licking; join Abraham Kellar; Daniel Morgan's line; cross Bowman's Creek; Autograph assessment of Charles Lee to James Nourse; wit. Thomas Lee.

Bundle 164.

No.	Name	Rank	Acres Surveyed		
	James Mercer	Field out. Col. Dunbar's,	1000	Dec. 21, 1785,	By John Veech, Jefferson Co., on s. bank of Ky. River, below Drenning's Lick Creek, ass'd to Samuel Beall, by John F. Mercer, heir to John Mercer, who was heir to James Mercer.
663. 664. 665.	Thomas Buford, dec'd. Thomas Buford, dec'd. Thomas Buford, dec'd.	Subaltern Byrd's, Subaltern Byrd's, Subaltern Washington's,	2000, 2000, 2000,	Jan. 11, 1786,	By Alexander D. Orr, Fayette Co., on the Ohio; cor. Francis Taylor; cor. Edward McGloughland; 14 miles below Big Sandy; to John Buford, heir-at-law to Thomas Buford; ass'd to Abraham Buford, by John Buford, Jr.
666. 667.	Thomas Buford, dec'd. Thomas Buford, dec'd.	Serg't Braddock's, Serg't Braddock's,	200, 200,		

Bundle 165—No. 2.

No.	Name	Acres	Surveyed	Description
249.	Christopher Hudson,	1000,	May 27, 1785,	By John Waller; Fayette Co., on Cabbin Creek, and on the old Indian road, about 5 or 6 miles from mouth of said creek. Ass'd to Lewis Craig; "This survey appears to have been made on part of a Military Warrant No. 249, granted to Christopher Hudson, and by him ass'd to Thomas Pollock, and by him to Lewis Craig and sent to the Register's office with another survey."
590.	Robert Goodwin,	Soldier Phillip's Co. 50,	Nov. 4, 1785,	By G. Calhoon, Nelson Co., on forks of Beech Fork and Chaplin's Fork; ass'd to John Crutchfield,

Bundle 166.

No.	Name	Rank	Acres	Surveyed	Description
822.	Hugh McNeill,	Drummer Throgmorton's Co.,	200,	Mar. 23, 1786,	By Isaac Cox, Nelson Co., on waters Cox's Creek, adj. Walter Baker and John Timberlaque; ass'd to John May.
737.	Adam Stephen,	Captain, Fry's,	3000,	Nov. 3, 1785,	By Richard Woolfolk, Nelson Co., on Ohio, below mouth of Salt River, at mouth of French Creek.

Bundle 167.

No. Warrant.	Name	Rank	Acres Surveyed	
228.	William Tutt,	Soldier,	50, June 30, 1785,	By John Watter, Fayette Co., on the Ohio; cor. Martin Nall; below Three Islands down river.
285.	James Granill.	Sergeant,	200, Oct. 5, 1785,	By Daniel Boone, Fayette Co., on main Licking, adj. Nathaniel Pope; ass'd to Joseph Watkins.
686.	Thomas Craddock.	Fifer.	200,	
687.	Bartlet Ford.	Soldier,	50,	
688.	Moses Parrish.	Soldier,	50,	
689.	William Blunkhall,	Corporal,	200,	
690.	Stephen Atkins,	Soldier,	50,	
691.	Charles Jordan,		200, Oct. 6, 1785,	By Daniel Boone, Fayette Co., adj. Joseph Watkins, on e. end; Ass'd to Thomas Watkins. [No Warrant.]
173.	William Stephenson,	Soldier,	50, [No Survey.]	Ass'd to Nathaniel Wilkinson.

Bundle 168.

No. Warrant.	Name	Rank	Acres Surveyed	
322.	Richard Hickman,	Sub. Stephen's,	1000, Nov. 11, 1785,	By John Helm, Nelson Co., on Ohio, opposite Blue River; cor. Robert Gilbert; cor. William Preston; Preston's Creek; to James Hickman, brother and heir-at-law.
323.	Richard Hickman,	Sub. Stephen's,	1000,	

Bundle 170.

No. Warrant.	Name	Rank	Acres Surveyed	
151.	Joseph Fox,	Capt. Indep. Co.,	1000, Nov. 18, 1783,	By William Roberts, Jefferson Co., James Patton's line; Ass'd to Capt. Meredith Price.
775.	Jacob Morris,	Sergeant,	200, Apr. 18, 1785,	By Daniel Sullivan, Jefferson Co., waters of Guesses Creek; cor. John Overton; cor. Nathan Reed.

Bundles 171–172.

No. Warrant.	Name	Rank	Acres Surveyed	
682.	Jacob Sharp,	Soldier,	50, Oct. 5, 1785,	By Daniel Boone, Fayette Co., on a small creek of the Licking, a little above the mouth of Flat Creek; ass'd to William Craddock; to Stith Gregory; to Bartholomew Dandridge; to John Pope; to Nathaniel Pope.
683.	Thomas Poo,	Soldier,	50,	

Bundles 171–172.

No. Warrant	Name	Rank	Acres	Surveyed	
684.	William Oglesby,	Soldier,	50,	Oct. 5, 1785,	Ass'd to Bartholomew Dandridge, to John Pope; to Nathaniel Pope.
685.	William Flanders,	Soldier,	50,	Oct. 5, 1785,	By Thomas Allin, Fayette Co., on Ohio, adj. Andrew Woods and Isaac Ware; to
250.	Richard Poindexter, dec'd,	Soldier,	50,	Apr. 21, 1785,	John Poindexter, Guardian to the co-heirs of Richard Poindexter; Ass'd to William Arnold; to Thomas Graves.
435.	James Ratliff,	Sold. Capt. Spotswood's,	50,	Apr. 21, 1785.	
446.	James Ratliff,	Sold. Capt. Phillips',	50,	Apr. 21, 1785.	
472.	James Ratliff,	Sold. Capt. Sam'l Overton's,	50,	Apr. 21, 1785.	
647.	James Goulding,	Soldier Byrd's,	50,	May 18, 1785,	By George Wilson, Jefferson Co., on waters of Fish Pool Creek; cor. John Pope; cor. James McCauley; Ass'd to Robert Goode; to William Bryan; to William Pope.
648.	Freeman Lewelling,	Sold. Byrd's,	50,	May 18, 1785,	By George Wilson, Jefferson Co., on waters of Fish Pool Creek; cor. Pope; Ass'd to Robert Goode; to William Bryan; to William Pope.
649.	Ed. Penix,	Sold. Byrd's,	50,		
167.	Martin Nall,	Soldier, Field's Co.,	50,	June 30, 1785,	By John Waller, Fayette Co., on the Ohio; cor. Robert Gilbert, below the three Islands.
235.	Arnold Steal,	Sergeant,	200,	June 6, 1787,	By James Garrard, Bourbon Co., on Licking; to include Upper Blue Licks; ass'd to William Preston and James Patton Preston.

Bundle 175–A.

No. Warrant	Name	Rank	Acres	Surveyed	
	Joseph Beckley,	Lieutenant,	2000,	July 16, 1774,	By Jno. Floyd, Fincastle Co., on waters of Elk Horn, on s. s.; cor. William Preston; cor. William Russell.

No. Warrant	Name	Rank	Acres Surveyed	
Bundle 175-A.				
181.	Simon Gillet,	Soldier,	50,	May 3, 1787, By Robert Breckinridge, Jefferson Co., on Ohio, below the Falls; adj. Warrenstaff, Bowyer and Byrd; cor. Thomas Hughes; Ass'd to John May; to Samuel Beall.
182.	David Poe,	Soldier,	50,	
189.	Matthew Roberts,	Soldier,	50,	
332.	James Hilling,	Soldier Byrd's,	50,	
Bundle 179.				
784.	George Mercer,	Field Off. Byrd's,	1000,	Nov. 3, 1785, By John Helm, Nelson Co., on Ohio, about 8 or 9 miles below Doe Run; adj. John May, at mouth of French Creek.
790.	George Mercer,	Capt. Washingt'n's,	1000,	
793.	George Mercer,	Captain Fry's,	1000,	
794.	George Mercer,	Captain Fry's,	1000,	
185.	Thomas Early,	Soldier,	50,	Jan. 30, 1787, By I. [or J.] Thomas, Surv. Mercer Co., Mercer; on Dick's River; cor. Peter Bellisfelt; cor. James Thompson; ass'd to Moses Dooley; to Samuel Shelton.
	William Sutherland,	Ensign 95th Foot,	1000,	May 4, 1774, By Hancock Taylor; Fincastle Co., on Ohio; about 30 miles below mouth of Scioto; Certificate of Lord Dunmore attached. [Fine.] No survey, to Overton Harris, heir-at-law; Ass'd to Frederick Harris, to Cyrus McCracken.
592.	Benjamin Harris,	Sold. Hudson's Co.,	50,	
1015	James McCollister,	Lieut. Pa. Regt.	1000,	July 26, 1784, By John Donelson, Lincoln Co. To Philip Pendleton, Ass'nee; Ass'd to George McCormack.
Bundle 180.				
779.	Nathan Holloway.	Soldier,	50,	Apr. 9, 1785, By James Morgan; Fayette Co., on waters of Hinkston's Fork; Richard Rixey's line; Ass'd to Frederick Raperton.
903.	James Board,	Soldier Byrd's,	50,	No Survey attached.
Bundles 181-182.				
1084.	Joseph Willis,	Sold. Dickenson's Co.,	50,	July 28, 1786, By Edward Willis, Lincoln Co., on waters of Salt R.; cor. David Adams.

No. Warrant	Name	Rank	Acres	Surveyed
	Bundle 183.			
	Burr Harrison,		2000,	June 25, 1774, By Hancock Taylor, Fincastle Co., on a fork of Elk Horn; cor. Hancock Taylor; Ass'd to Gabriel Jones; Certificate of Lord Dunmore.
341.	Capt. Charles Lewis,	Captain,	1000,	Feb. 12, 178-, By Charles Morgan, Fayette Co., on waters of Boone's Creek and Elk Lick branch; cor. Benjamin Logan; to William Lewis, Ex'r.
771.	John Dickinson Littlepage,	Subaltern,	2000,	Dec. 17, 1785, By J. F. Moore, Jefferson Co., on Drenning's Lick Creek, about 6 miles above the Lick; cor. Charles Minn Thruston.
	John Blagg,	Captain [3000],	1000,	June 7, 1774, By Jno. Floyd, Fincastle Co., on waters of Bear Grass; forks of Bear Grass about 5 miles from Falls; cor. Southall and Charleton.
	Bundle 184.			
103.	Richard Parker,	Soldier Byrd's,	50,	Nov. 9, 1785, By Charles Ewing, Nelson, on n. s. Beech Fork; cor. Richard Nall; cor. William Harrod; ass'd to Isaac McCarty.
301.	Alexander Finnie,	Lieut. Capt De-Peroney's Co.,	2000,	Dec. 16, 1784, By John Handley, Jefferson Co., in Forks of Green River and Panther Creek; Chilton's line; cor. Jacob Myers; to William Finnie, heir-at-law; Ass'd to John May.
180.	Henry Bolton,	Soldier,	50,	Oct. 16, 1786, By Ro. Breckinridge, Jefferson Co., on first island in the Ohio above Diamond Island, generally called Eighteen-Mile Island.
316.	Reuben Munday,	Soldier,	50,	Nov. 16, 1785, By Ro. Breckinridge, Nelson Co., on Rolling Fork; adj. Terrel and Hawkins.

Bundle 194.

No. Warrant	Name	Rank	Acres Surveyed	
692.	Joseph Stevens,	Field Off. [3000],	2000,	Nov. 29, 1783, By Alex'r Breckenridge, Jefferson Co., on headwaters of Beurgrass, adj. land of Edmund Taylor and John Ashby.
852.	William Brock,	Soldier Stephen's,	50,	
853.	Littleberry Lane,	Soldier Byrd's,	50,	Feb. 1, 1787, By Charles Smith, Deputy to James Garrard, S. B. C.; Bourbon Co., on Hinkston's Mill Creek; cor. Burnley & Smith. McMillion's; all assigned to Chas. Smith.
855.	Patrick Fisher,	Serg't Byrd's,	200,	
856.	Basil Goodman,	Sold. Capt. Bullitt's Co.,	50,	
857.	John Dolton,	Sold. Capt. Thos. Bullitt's Co.,	50,	
858.	Peter Clarkson,	Sold. Sam Overton's Co.,	50,	

Bundle 195.

No. Warrant	Name	Rank	Acres Surveyed	
641	James Taylor,	Sub. Hogg's Co.,	2000,	June 24, 1785, By Arch'd Campbell, Fayette Co., on Boon's Creek, adj. David Robinson; crossing Floyd's Fork, a branch of Boon's Creek; Ass'd to John Floyd, by Edmund Taylor, Att'y. Apr. 29, 1780.

Bundle 202.

No. Warrant	Name	Rank	Acres Surveyed	
294.	Dr. Thomas Loyd,	Serjeant,	200,	Mar. 21, 1789, By C. Worley, Fayette Co., Forks of Elkhorn; adjoins Gen'l Lewis.

Bundle 203.

No. Warrant	Name	Rank	Acres Surveyed	
989.	Dr. James Craik,	Lieutenant,	2000,	Sept. 10, 1788, By George Reading, Jr., Deputy to James Garrard, S. B. C.; Bourbon Co., on a fork on Indian Creek. Surveyed for James Craig

No. Warrant.	Name	Rank	Acres	Surveyed	

Bundle 203.

| 702. | William Peachy, | Field Off. Frontier Battalion, | 5000, | Mar. 20, 1784, | By Robert Johnson, Fayette Co., on Licking; cor. Pretimon Merry [Prettyman Merry]; at a branch running into the Ohio, about 1 mile below mouth of Licking; Dry Creek; Bank Lick; cor. Joseph Davis. [Letters attached.] |
| | Walter Cunningham, | Lieutenant, | 1000, | Nov. 12, 1775, | By I. Hite, Fincastle Co., on Clear Creek; [Certificate of Lord Dunmore attached.] |

Bundle 204.

| 68. | John Shelby, | | 1000, | Nov. 19, 1788, | By Wm McBrayer, Deputy to John Thomas, S. M. C.; Mercer Co., on branches of Chaplin's Fork; cor. to Harbison. |
| 505. | James Lloyd, | Sergeant Byrd's, | 200, | Dec. 15, 1785, | By Charles Ewing, Deputy to Will May, S. N. C.; Nelson; near Wilson's Station. |

Bundle 205.

| 975. | Joseph Beckley, | Lieut. Capt. William Phillips' Co., | 2000, | June 16, 1787, | By Jonathan Longstreth, Deputy to James French, S. M. C.; Madison; on Station Camp Creek; joins Nathaniel Alexander; cor. James Stevenson. |

Bundles 206–207.

| 456. | John Jones, | Drummer Byrd's, | 200, | Mar. 27, 1781, | By Hubbard Taylor, Lincoln Co., on waters of Paint Lick and Gilbert's Creek. |

Bundles 208–209.

| 715. | Lemuel Barnett, | Captain, | 1000, | June 25, 1788, | By G. Calhoon, Deputy to Will May, S. N. C.; Nelson; on waters of Pottinger's Creek; near Kinchlow's Cabbin; ass'd to John Lindsey. |

Bundle 214.

NO. Warrant,	NAME	RANK	ACRES SURVEYED	
551.	Richard Martin,	Soldier Capt. Morderni Buckner's Co.,	50,	Jan. 26, 1787, By George King, Nelson; on Froman's Creek; adj. Gabriel May; ass'd to Abner May; to Humphrey May.
552.	John Perrie,	Serg't Capt. John McNeal's Co.,	200,	
554. 555.	Francis Roberts, Benjamin Clements,	Sold. McNeal's Co., Soldier Capt. William Temple's Co.,	50, 50,	
551.	Richard Martin,	Soldier Capt. Mordecai Buckner's Co.,	50,	Jan. 26, 1787, By George King, Nelson Co., on Froman's Creek; adj. Gabriel May; Ass'd to Abner May; to Humphrey May.
552.	John Perrie,	Serg't Capt. John McNeal's Co.;	200,	
554.	Francis Roberts,	Sold. Capt. John McNeal's Co.,	50,	
555.	Benjamin Clements,	Sold. Capt. William Temple's Co.,	50,	
783.	Charles Bowles,	Soldier Byrd's,	50,	Sept. 25, 1787, By John Helm, Nelson Co., on Beech Fork and Rolling Fork; adj. Betty Roberts; Ass'd to Samuel Meredith.
877. 878. 879. 881. 747. 748. 749. 750. 1166.	William Dean, Martin Howlet, William Murrell, Alexander Stewart, Samuel Bentley, James Owen, John Osbourn, Richard Griffin, John Furrer, William McGehee,	Non-com., Non-com., Non-com., Non-com., Soldier, Soldier, Soldier, Soldier, Serjeant, Soldier Phillips',	200, 200, 200, 200, 50, 50, 50, 50, 200, 50,	May 11, 1784, By Matthew Walton, Jefferson Co., on Beech Fork and Hardin's Creek; Nall's line; Norris's line.
559.	William Foster,	Sold. Capt. Sam Overton's Co.,	50,	May 11, 1784, By Matthew Walton, Jefferson Co., on Hardin's Creek; Ezekiel Norris's line; Ass'd to William McGehee.

No. Warrant.	Name	Rank	Acres	Surveyed	
	Bundle 215.				
405	Jeremiah Self,	Serjeant,	200,	July 29, 1786,	By John Price, Lincoln Co., on waters of Gilbert's, Paint Lick and Sugar Creeks; cor. Craig; near Boon's old trace; Ass'd to William Arnold; to Lewis Craig.
	Richard Four [?],	Soldier,	50,	Sept. 4, 1786,	By Arch'd Campbell, Fayette Co., on middle fork of Glen's Creek.
	James Arnold,	Soldier,	50,		
	Alexander Boyd,	Lieutenant,	2000,	July 14, 1774,	By John Floyd, Fincastle Co., on branches of Elk Horn, on s. s., about 105 miles from the Ohio; cor. John Carter; William Phillips' line; to Andrew Boyd, heir-at-law of Alexander Boyd, dec'd.
	Bundles 219-220.				
133.	James Johnson,	Serjeant Capt. John Burton's Co.,	200,	Sept. 20, 1787,	By John Helm, Nelson Co., on n. s. Beech Fork; adj. Samuel Meredith; Froman's Creek; Ass'd to John Hightower; to his son, William Hightower.
435.	James Cooper,	Soldier Byrd's,	50,	Feb. 7, 1786,	By Richard Young, Fayette Co., on Ky. River, about 4 miles above Leestown; John Price's line; cor. John Craig; Ass'd to James Haydon.
448.	James Tinder,	Soldier Byrd's,	50,		
484.	William Ross,	Private,	50,		
616.	James Riddle,	Non-com. Capt. Hogg's,	50,	May 29, 1786,	By Richard Young, Fayette Co., on Ky. River, at the old ford, 30 poles below mouth of Hickman's Creek; Ass'd to Zachariah Herndon.
617.	James Riddle,	Non-com. Capt. Hogg's,	50,		
	Bundles 221-222.				
949.	Charles Ellison,	Corp. Capt. Root's Co. Rangers,	200,	May 28, 1789,	By James Cox, Nelson Co., on middle branch of Cedar Creek that the Buffaloe road crosses, that goes from Cox's Creek to Salt River garrison.

No. Warrant.	Name	Rank	Acres Surveyed	
Bundle 226.				
583.	James Ward, dec'd,	Sub. Col. Boquet's Independent Regt.	400,	Nov. 25, 1784, By William Henry, Fayette Co., on north fork of Licking, adj. William Bickley's settlement on South, Angus Cameron on the west; Ass'd to William Ward, heir-at-law.
584.	James Ward,		400,	
585.	James Ward,		400,	
586.	James Ward,		400,	
587.	James Ward,		400,	
923.	David Robinson,	Sub. Capt. Alexander Sayers' Co.,	2000,	Apr. 12, 1784, By W. Ward, Fayette Co., on n. e. fork of Licking; Ass'd to William Ward, of Botetourt.
Bundle 227.				
954.	John Tredway,	Soldier Gist's Co.,	50,	Jan. 26, 1786, By William Steele, Fayette Co., on waters of Hickman's Creek; William Kennedy's line; Embly's line; cor. Samuel Martin.
955.	Benjamin Cage,	Sold. Capt. Richard Dogget's Co.,	50,	
1195.	Joseph Wooten,	Soldier 2d Va.,	50,	
1196.	Joseph Wooten,	Soldier 2d Va.,	50,	
Bundle 232.				
	William Long,	Lieut. Va. Levies,	2000,	Apr. 13, 1785, By Richard Woolfolk, Jefferson Co., on waters of Bullskin Creek; adj. Samuel Beall; crossing Clear Creek; Ass'd to William Strother Madison.
Bundle 233.				
778.	William McCormick,	Sub. Col. Boquet's Rangers,	200,	Dec. 23, 1785, By Benoni Swearingen, Fayette Co., on s. s. of s. fork of Licking; about 4 miles above fork.
Bundles 235–236.				
1019.	William Tinsley,	Soldier Byrd's,	50,	Mar. 10, 1788, By Charles Ewing, Nelson Co., on Hardin's Creek.
526.	Charles Travis,	Drummer,	200,	Mar. 23, 1787, By Ja. McCoun, Jr., Mercer Co., on first large Buffaloe road that crosses Kentucky River, below mouth of Little Benson Creek.

No. Warrant,	Name	Rank	Acres Surveyed
	Bundles 235-236.		
342.	John McMahon,	Soldier,	50, Oct. 21. 1786, By Rob. Breckinridge, Deputy to Alex'r Breckinridge, Jefferson Co., on Ohio, below John Campbell's Military survey; Ass'd to Thomas Hughes; to Robert Breckinridge.
	Bundles 244-245.		
206.	William Skillern,	Serjeant,	200, June 30, 1786, By W. Montgomery, Lincoln Co., on Givens's Run; cor. John Dougherty; cor. Andrew Dodd.
	Bundles 246-247.		
	Angus McDonald,		2000, July 7, 1774, By Hancock Taylor, Fincastle Co., on Elk Horn; cor. William Peachy; to John and Angus McDonald, sons and devisees.
	Bundles 267-268.		
870.	William Davis,	Soldier,	50, Nov. 19, 1784, By Green Clay, Lincoln Co., on waters of Sugar Creek; Scott's hunting park.
	Bundles 269-270.		
365.	George Muse,	Field Officer,	1000, June 8, 1785, By Thomas Allin, Fayette Co., on Ohio River, about 700 poles above mouth of Licking; Ass'd to James Taylor.
389. 372. 373.	George Muse, George Muse, George Muse,	Field Officer, Field Officer, Field Officer,	500, 500, 500, June 8, 1785, By Thomas Allin, Fayette Co., on the forks between the Licking and Ohio; Ass'd to James Taylor. [This is now Newport, Ky.]
1200.	John Montgomery,	Soldier,	50, No survey found.
	Bundles 271-272.		
429.	William Kernal,	Soldier Byrd's,	50, Oct. 10, 1784, By Richard Young, Fayette Co., on waters of Elk Horn, on the Sink Hole Ground. Cor. Taylor Nowell.

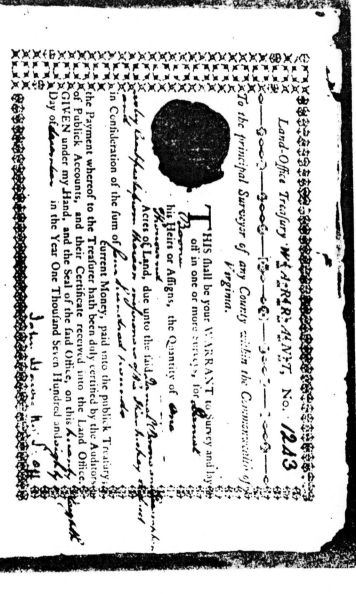

Land-Office Treasury WARRANT, No. 1243

To the principal Surveyor of any County within the Commonwealth of Virginia.

THIS shall be your WARRANT to survey and lay off in one or more Surveys, for _____ his Heirs or Assigns, the Quantity of one _____ Acres of Land, due unto the said _____ in Consideration of the Sum of _____ current Money, paid into the publick Treasury; the Payment whereof to the Treasurer hath been duly certified by the Auditors of Publick Accounts, and their Certificate received unto the Land Office. GIVEN under my Hand, and the Seal of the said Office, on this _____ Day of _____ in the Year One Thousand Seven Hundred and _____

John Harvie

The Plat was laid down by a Scale of
200 Poles to the Inch

D — A
Area 400 Acres
No 1975

No 1976
Area 1000 Acres

N
C — B

Fayette County Aug't 29 1783

Surveyed for Daniel Boone 400 Acres
of Land by virtue of a Certificate for Settlement on the Waters of
Stoners Fork of Licking, duly entered
January 17th 1780 Beginning at A
a Walnut, Poplar and Cherry Tree
Thence S 160 P crossing a Branch to
B a Linn and Small Hickery, thence
W 400 P Including a Spring at an
old Camp on the North Side of the
Branch and some Bushes cut, to C a Poplar Linn and Sugar Tree
thence N 160 P to D a Poplar and small Sugar Tree, thence E 400 P
crossing the aforesaid Branch to the Beginning

Fayette County Aug't 29th 1783

Surveyed for Daniel Boone 1000 Acres of Land by Virtue of a
Preemption Warrant No 1243 duly Entered No 7 December 1782, Lying on a
bank on the South of his Settlement Beginning at A a Linn and Small
Hickory a corner to the Settlement, thence S 400 P to B a Linn Hickory and
Sugar Tree, thence W 400 P to C a Buckeye Linn and Hickory Tree,
thence N 400 P crossing a Branch to D a Poplar Linn, and Sugar Tree
Corner with the Settlement, thence E along the Settlement line 400 P
to the Beginning

Kilis Moore }
Abm Scholl } Chain-Men

William Scholl Marker

William Hays D.S.

Tho' Marshall C.C.

I do Certify that Daniel Boone ...
... land ...
... Timber & of Green... Brown ...
William Shull B...
his mark ...

...
...
...
... I have given over all my right of the
with plat to William Shull for
the sum ... of ... Green Boys ...
August 1784
... Daniel Boone

1200 Acres Surveyed
Aug. 29th 1783

Recd Feb 25
27 August 84
...
Wm Shull
Grant ... 15
July 1785
recorded
page
146

Index of Persons in "Earliest Surveys of Land in Kentucky."